# PRAISE FOR *LOVING WE*

"With our world feeling more divi[...] book holds a key for changing hearts, minds, and stories. *Loving Well in a Broken World* is a humble but challenging book with the great possibility to heal. If you have felt despair or hopelessness, Lauren's book is a manifesto and guide for rising to the questions of our time with love and faith and hope"

—Sarah Bessey, author of *Miracles and Other Reasonable Things* and *Jesus Feminist*

"*Loving Well in a Broken World* is a powerful and spirited manifesto. Lauren Casper challenges us to break out of our shells and revisit what it means to truly "love our neighbors." With insight and infectious passion, Casper pushes us to see and embrace empathy in a new way, encouraging us to overcome the ills that often hold us back from loving others with abandon."

—Matthew Paul Turner, author of *When God Made You* and *When I Pray for You*

"Lauren Casper is at her best in this book. Her writing is vulnerable, vivid, and ultimately deeply convicting. She shows us that when we open our hearts to others, not only does it make the world a better place, but we often discover the truest version of ourselves as well."

—Jen Fulwiler, bestselling author of *One Beautiful Dream* and SiriusXM radio host

"In a world where division and 'us' versus 'them' seems to be growing out of control, Lauren Casper reminds the reader of the lost art of empathy and the power it has to unify and create an 'us for them' mentality. *Loving Well in a Broken World* is a book I hope everyone reads because it reminds us how to do just that."

—Heather Avis, bestselling author and narrative shifter

"*Loving Well in a Broken World* is a gift to the church. Lauren discusses the impossibility of love that is made possible only through seeing and knowing our neighbor, by believing with and for them. In creating the curriculum on how to love, Lauren generously offers up moments of grief, despair, and longing from her own life, allowing her vulnerability to be part of our education. This book anchors the most frustrating, debilitating parts of loving others to the one thing that could make it all worth it: hope. The Bible's simplest commands are often the hardest to keep, but *Loving Well in a Broken World* provides essential tools to help us along the way."

—Joy Beth Smith, author of *Party of One*

"Lauren Casper urges us not to settle for fracture when flourishing waits past the edges of our comfort. Bold, luminous, and pulsing with possibility, this book offers the permission we need to trade our fears for the promise of connection. I'm cheering wildly for this one."

—Shannan Martin, author of *The Ministry of Ordinary Places* and *Falling Free*

"It is the answer to our division, the secret to effective leadership, essential to loving our neighbors, and yet a shockingly overlooked practice. *Empathy* is one of the most underestimated tools in our spiritual tool belt, but through her story telling, self-reflection, and biblical insight, Lauren Casper makes the case for its transformative power. We are a people and a church in desperate need of empathy, which is why I truly believe each of us needs this book. I sure did."

—Sharon Hodde Miller, author of *Nice: Why We Love to Be Liked and How God Calls Us to More*

"In a world where we are more connected than ever, yet struggle to really bear one another's burdens in love, Lauren shares with us her hard-won secret to this problem: deciding that if something affects our neighbor, it affects us too. We are daily confronted with stories of pain, sadness, and injustice and it can be easy to feel overwhelmed and powerless. This book will empower you to truly love your neighbor, even the ones you haven't met yet."

—Taylor Schumann, writer and contributor
to *If I Don't Make It, I Love You*

"Lauren Casper's *Loving Well in a Broken World* is a kind but firm reminder of what we are called to do: care for one another with empathy and love while navigating this world. Using personal experience and relatable storytelling, Lauren helps us learn how to take a walk in someone else's shoes. This book is a must-read."

—Rachel Von Stein, writer, speaker, and advocate

"Lauren Casper leads us on a journey to discover what might happen when we start to look at things differently. We're all longing for a deep connection with others in these divided times, and through her captivating story Casper helps us realize this is possible and—as it feels urgently important—she shows us how. What a gift!"

—Hayley Morgan, author of *Preach to Yourself*
and coauthor of *Wild and Free*

"*Loving Well in a Broken World* is a book meant to help us each restore the covenant in our own hearts. We are to love God and love each other. Lauren Casper eloquently helps the reader believe that they can find the strength to love again, even when it hurts."

—Dr. Heather Thompson Day, author,
communication professor, and speaker

"It's the thing so many of us are trying to do—love those around us while living in a world that is not as it should be. However, I don't want to listen to just anyone on this topic; I want to hear from the people doing the awkward, difficult, service-centered work of loving their neighbors. Lauren Casper is one of today's trusted voices in pursuit of empathy. In *Loving Well in a Broken World*, Lauren shares both personal mishaps and poignant lessons, giving her credibility and endearing her to the reader. The world needs more of the life laid out in this book. May we read it and follow Lauren's lead."

—**Alexandra Kuykendall**, author of *Loving My Actual Neighbor* and cofounder of *The Open Door Sisterhood*

# LOVING
# WELL
# IN A
# BROKEN
# WORLD

# LOVING WELL IN A BROKEN WORLD

## DISCOVER THE HIDDEN POWER OF EMPATHY

### LAUREN CASPER

Published in Nashville, Tennessee, by Nelson Books, an imprint of Thomas Nelson. Nelson Books and Thomas Nelson are registered trademarks of HarperCollins Christian Publishing, Inc.

The author is represented by Alive Literary Agency, 7680 Goddard Street, Suite 200, Colorado Springs, Colorado 80920, www.aliveliterary.com.

Thomas Nelson titles may be purchased in bulk for educational, business, fund-raising, or sales promotional use. For information, please e-mail SpecialMarkets@ThomasNelson.com.

Unless otherwise noted, Scripture quotations are taken from the ESV® Bible (The Holy Bible, English Standard Version®). Copyright © 2001 by Crossway, a publishing ministry of Good News Publishers. Used by permission. All rights reserved.

Scripture quotations marked CEB are from the Common English Bible. Copyright © 2011 Common English Bible.

Scripture quotations marked KJV are from the King James Version. Public domain.

Scripture quotations marked THE MESSAGE are from *The Message*. Copyright © by Eugene H. Peterson 1993, 1994, 1995, 1996, 2000, 2001, 2002. Used by permission of NavPress. All rights reserved. Represented by Tyndale House Publishers, Inc.

Scripture quotations marked NASB are from New American Standard Bible®. Copyright © 1960, 1962, 1963, 1968, 1971, 1972, 1973, 1975, 1977, 1995 by The Lockman Foundation. Used by permission. (www.Lockman.org)

Scripture quotations marked NIV are from the Holy Bible, New International Version®, NIV®. Copyright © 1973, 1978, 1984, 2011 by Biblica, Inc.® Used by permission of Zondervan. All rights reserved worldwide. www.Zondervan.com. The "NIV" and "New International Version" are trademarks registered in the United States Patent and Trademark Office by Biblica, Inc.®

Scripture quotations marked NLT are from the Holy Bible, New Living Translation. © 1996, 2004, 2007, 2013, 2015 by Tyndale House Foundation. Used by permission of Tyndale House Publishers, Inc., Carol Stream, Illinois 60188. All rights reserved.

Scripture quotations marked NRSV are from New Revised Standard Version Bible. Copyright © 1989 National Council of the Churches of Christ in the United States of America. Used by permission. All rights reserved.

ISBN 978-0-7180-8559-9 (eBook)
ISBN 978-0-7180-8555-1 (TP)

Library of Congress Control Number: 2019953526

*Printed and bound by CPI Group (UK) Ltd, Croydon, CR0 4YY*

20 21 22 23 24  LSC  10 9 8 7 6 5 4 3

*For John*

# CONTENTS

# CONTENTS

# A WAY BACK TO LOVE

If we are to love our neighbors, before doing anything
else we must see our neighbors. With our imagination as
well as our eyes, that is to say like artists, we must see not
just their faces but the life behind and within their faces.
Here it is love that is the frame we see them in.
FREDERICK BUECHNER, *WHISTLING IN THE DARK*

S ometimes people are just so *mean*!" The words tumble
out of my seven-year-old's mouth, punctuated by a sob
that catches in his throat.

I stare back into large brown eyes framed by thick, wet
lashes and feel my heart lurch. I wish I could snap my fingers
and fix the world for him.

"Yes, that's true," I agree. "Sometimes people are
really mean."

His tears come with more force. Perhaps he hoped I
would tell him he is wrong—that people aren't mean, and
maybe he misunderstood the kids on the playground—but I

don't. Instead, I think about all the times I've been shut down or shut out, all the times I've been teased or harassed . . . or worse. I can't tell him people aren't mean and the world is lovely, because sometimes people are awful and the world isn't a pleasant place to be.

I rub his back and begin to tell him a few stories from my own childhood, a time that wasn't terrible overall but had its hard moments—braces, glasses, anxiety, epilepsy, a truly awful haircut, and insecurity. I tell him about being afraid when I saw scary stories on the news about bad people who'd committed crimes in our city. His tears slow, and he stares back at me. I reiterate, "Sometimes the world is mean, and it feels awful."

His face crumples again and he cries against my chest, "What are we going to do?"

The question is thousands of years old, but the answer, given by a wise teacher, still holds true . . .

*Love your neighbor as yourself.*

I say it softly.

"But *how*?!" he wails, and I feel every bit of his confusion and fear deep in my bones.

His question is one I regularly ask myself. How *do* we love our neighbors in a cruel world? How do we respond when anger breathes fire in our face? How, oh how, do we turn our second cheek when the first is still burning from being slapped?

The temptation is always to circle the wagons, gather our friends close, and lock the doors. Maybe if we close our eyes and ears to the outside world, we can cocoon ourselves within a community that believes and looks and acts just like we do, and we'll call the people in it our neighbors. Then it won't cost us a thing to love our neighbors as ourselves, because we'll barely be able to distinguish between our neighbors and ourselves.

But how best to circle the wagons is not the question my son is asking. He isn't seeking an easy way out; he wants to know the practical how-to. He wants to know how to love others in a world that sometimes greets a hug with a punch and a greeting with a curse.

My son wants to know what it looks like to love on the playground when bullies taunt him and tell him he doesn't belong because of the color of his skin. And I wonder what it looks like to love in the coffee shop, in the pews, and on Main Street when confederate flags line the sidewalks downtown. He wonders how to love when another kid breaks his toy, and I want to know how to love when another person breaks my heart. We both want to stop all the pain and the brutality, but we can't. So how do we live and love in the midst of it?

I think it starts with resisting that knee-jerk temptation to circle the wagons. Instead of closing ourselves off, we can dive heart-first into the mess, wrap our arms around each other, and climb out together. In a world gone mad, we can choose to stay in the thick of it and love our way to the other side. We can seek understanding. We can be *with* instead of *against*. We can identify our blind spots and ask questions when we don't understand someone else's point of view. We can approach life with humility and courage, leaning into our discomfort and big feelings instead of denying them. We can live and love in a broken world by running toward this thing called empathy.

*Empathy*—to see another's pain, understand the cause of it, and then feel with them.

The myth of empathy is that it requires shared experience. I don't believe that's true. While it certainly requires more work to empathize with those whose journeys differ from our own, it isn't impossible. It simply requires our effort and a real desire to learn. We may have to look more carefully, expand our worldview, open our ears and homes and hearts, but we can empathize with others, regardless of our differences. We can choose to set aside our fears, judgments, and stereotypes. We *can* do this. And once we do, we will have taken our first steps on the path to loving our neighbors as ourselves.

Jesus, our wise teacher, said it this way: "You shall love the Lord your God with all your heart and with all your soul and with all your mind. This is the great and first commandment. And a second is like it: You shall love your neighbor as yourself. On these two commandments depend all the Law and the Prophets" (Matthew 22:37–40).

Sometimes the simplest answers are the hardest answers. When everything is falling apart and the world around us is in chaos and we want to know what our part in the solution should be, we instinctively know the answer. The secular world calls it the "Golden Rule," and the world's major faith groups agree on their own version of it.

In 1993, a declaration drafted by Dr. Hans Küng was presented to the Parliament of the World's Religions in Chicago, Illinois. He called it "Towards a Global Ethic: An Initial Declaration," and over two hundred faith leaders from over forty world religions signed their endorsement.[1] Since then, thousands of other faith leaders and global citizens have signed their agreement to this declaration that states, "We must not live for ourselves alone, but should also serve others, never forgetting the children, the aged, the poor, the suffering, the disabled, the refugees, and the lonely. . . . We commit ourselves to this global ethic, to understanding one another, and . . . We invite all people, whether religious or not, to do the same."[2]

A quarter of a century has passed since the declaration was first presented and agreed upon by people from every faith and walk of life. We've seen global terrorism rise, human trafficking continue, and economies rise and fall and totally collapse. We've seen genocide, civil wars and foreign wars, refugees board overcrowded boats that capsize at sea, and children wash up on the shores of Greece and even our own borders. We've seen gun violence overtake our schools and homes and streets and malls and movie theaters and churches. Racism continues to infect minds and hearts, and hate still kills. The world is in crisis today, just as it was twenty-five years ago, and still we look to our left and right and ask ourselves, *How do I live in this mess? What is my role?*

We need to go back to Jesus' words: love God and love your neighbor.

Just love. It's the answer to everything—all our hurts, problems, divides. So why is it so hard to do? Why is the command to love so easily overlooked? How do we justify our tendency to respond instead with judgment, hate, discrimination, or even apathy? How do we get it so wrong? The clue lies right there in the verse, as we're called to "love your neighbor as yourself."

Loving our neighbor as ourselves is so much more than just asking, in any given situation, *What would I want in this scenario?* We know precisely what we'd want, because we have walked around in our own skin our entire lives. We know our own hopes, dreams, fears, disappointments, and hurts intimately. We know what touches our hearts, and we also know how to erect walls to keep out the pain. We've walked a lifetime in our own shoes. But loving our neighbor as ourselves requires a barefoot moment, a vulnerable stepping out of the known into the unknown so we can walk around for a while in someone else's sneakers. To truly understand what it is they want, need, hope for, feel and, therefore, how to love them in that.

Empathy. That's the often-overlooked key to it all. As we get to know each other, see one another, and hear one another, one person at a time, we will one day find our way back to love.

# ONE

# THE ANTIDOTE TO INDIFFERENCE

The opposite of love is not hate, it's indifference.
ELIE WIESEL

The story is told in the tenth chapter of Luke. Jesus is somewhere between the Sea of Galilee and Jerusalem, and a crowd has gathered to listen to him teach. In the crowd is a young lawyer who is eager to put Jesus to the test. When his chance comes, the lawyer steps forward and asks, "Teacher, what shall I do to inherit eternal life?" (v. 25).

Instead of answering directly, Jesus asks the lawyer what he thinks the answer might be.

The lawyer responds, "You shall love the Lord your God with all your heart and with all your soul and with all your strength and with all your mind, and your neighbor as yourself" (v. 27). Simple.

"You have answered correctly," Jesus says, and then adds, "do this and you will live" (v. 28).

But the lawyer, intent on justifying himself—intent on finding a reason *not* to do this—asks a follow-up question, "And who is my neighbor?" (v. 29). The lawyer knows the answer but is hoping for a loophole. His issue isn't a lack of knowledge or understanding, but a lack of love.

If we're honest, I think most of us also know the answer to the lawyer's question. In today's ever-connected world, we know the definition of neighbor isn't limited by geography. We know it could be anyone from the person next door to our colleagues at work, the laborer in the next state, the refugees at the border, the inmate in the county jail, the addict in rehab, the officer patrolling the inner city, and the sweatshop worker across the ocean. And yet, along with the lawyer, we want a shortcut or a way out from loving our neighbors as ourselves. We want a loophole, because loving others as we love our own hearts, minds, souls, and bodies can be hard and costly.

So, what follow-up question would a twenty-first-century person ask Jesus at this point? Maybe the same question my son asked through his tears: "But how?" How do we love others when everything from faith to ethnicity to politics to economics to education to social systems seems to divide us? Jesus' response to the young lawyer's "Who is my neighbor?" also provides a perfect answer to our "But how?"

Jesus' response is the parable of the good Samaritan.

As the story goes, a Jewish man is traveling by foot from Jericho to Jerusalem when he falls victim to a brutal mugging. He is robbed, stripped, and beaten within an inch of his life. A traveling priest notices the wounded man, but quickly moves to the other side of the road to pass by. A little later, a Levite approaches, sees the bloodied body in the street, and he, too, hurries by. Then a third man, a Samaritan, approaches, and this time the narrative shifts. His heart goes out to the man in the gutter and, instead of avoiding him, the Samaritan gently cleans and dresses the man's wounds. He carefully lifts the man onto his own animal and takes him to an inn where he continues to nurse the man back to health. When the Samaritan has to leave, he pays the innkeeper to continue caring for the man until he can return and finish caring for him himself.

There are four men in this story: the Jewish man who is mugged, the Jewish priest, the Levite, and the Samaritan. When Jesus finishes telling the story, he asks the lawyer, "Which of these three, do you think, proved to be a neighbor to the man who fell among the robbers?" (v. 36).

To which the lawyer responds, "The one who showed mercy" (v. 37). The Samaritan.

Jesus says, "You go and do likewise." In other words, "Exactly! Now, go and love like that guy!"

Jesus doesn't define who is and isn't a neighbor, because it's fairly obvious who our neighbor is—everyone. Instead, he tells a story about how to love well.

First, he lays out the *don't* list. Don't rob, beat, and strip your neighbor. (Obviously.) Don't rush by, ignore, or avoid the pain of others. Don't pretend people aren't hurting and dying. Don't be too busy, too prejudiced, too arrogant, or too ignorant to love others. *Don't be indifferent.*

Then he lays out the *do* list. Do notice others in their

pain. Do care. Do stop. Do go out of your way. Do spend your time, energy, emotions, and resources to help where there is need. Do check on others. Do see the people around you and choose to get involved. *Do love your neighbor.*

What would an ordinary, everyday parable of the good Samaritan look like today? Perhaps it would look something like what I experienced in the parking lot of a grocery store on a warm spring day several years ago.

I was tired, hurried, frustrated, and ready to go home. My husband, John, was just behind me, pushing our then two-year-old son, Mareto, in the grocery cart. We were moving as fast as we could, trying to make it to the parking lot before Mareto's meltdown got worse. I was frantically trying to open a cereal bar in an effort to stem the tears. Our then ten-month-old daughter, Arsema, was strapped to my chest in the Ergobaby carrier watching it all through wide eyes. Sweat beads were forming on my forehead, caused in part by my embarrassment, but mostly because I was hurrying through Trader Joe's with an eighteen-pound baby strapped to my chest.

I sure didn't feel like I was in the running for any mom-of-the-year awards. I felt like a hot mess. In fact, I was sincerely hoping no one was looking at us too closely . . . that somehow we were invisible to the people bustling around us. It was chaotic, exhausting, and, unfortunately, an all-too-common experience for us.

Our family doesn't exactly blend in. Not only are we white parents with two black children—something that causes enough stares and questions all by itself—but our children have both physical and developmental disabilities.

Which is to say, when we all go out together, we stand out. Sometimes, I don't mind—I'm proud of my family. My children are beautiful and, even with all its broken pieces and jagged edges, so is our story.

Other times, though, on the days when we are very far from having it together, I do mind. Those are the days I want to blend in with the crowd and escape the curious stares. Some days, I just want to be a family. Not the adoptive family. Not the family with special-needs. Not the unique family . . . just a family. This was one of those days.

I was close to tears myself as I rushed through the doors with Arsema on my chest. I was hoping to get to the car as quickly as possible when a voice behind me slowed my steps.

"Ma'am!" the woman called out. I hoped and prayed I wasn't the ma'am she was referring to.

"Ma'am!" the woman called out again.

When I stopped and turned, a young woman rushed toward me. A bright smile covered her face, and I immediately noticed her beautiful black curls, just like the black curls of the babe snuggled on my chest. I could see by the woman's shirt that she worked at the grocery store, and I assumed I must have dropped something.

"I just wanted you to have this bouquet," she said, holding out a colorful bunch of cut flowers. "I couldn't help but notice your family," she said, still smiling. "You remind me of my own family." She explained that she too had been adopted, and she saw herself in my daughter and her parents in John and me.

Somehow, she saw past it all—past the tears, the sweat, and the frazzled mess. Instead of failure, she saw a mom trying her best. Instead of a mess, she saw beauty in one of our real family moments.

She handed me the flowers, and I managed to choke out a thank you.

"Really," I said, "this means the world to me."

She patted my shoulder, told me my family was beautiful, and walked back into the store.

My steps were much slower as I turned around and headed to the car, my cheeks wet with tears.

She didn't know I was in the middle of some of the hardest days I'd known as a mother. She didn't know our son had recently been diagnosed with autism, that we were just months into new therapies and medications, and were completely overwhelmed with setting up services and support. She didn't know we were preparing our infant daughter for her first of several major surgeries, and that, as much as I tried to present a brave and optimistic face to those around us, I was terrified. She didn't know we were still feeling very uncertain of ourselves as parents in a transracial family. She didn't know any of that. She simply saw us and cared.

A couple of years later, I was able to reconnect with my grocery-store good Samaritan. Her friends and family call her JoJo. She is a single mother raising a son with special needs who is close in age to my own little boy. When she saw us in the store that day, she said she felt a connection—she knew something about what life was like for us. So she grabbed a bunch of flowers and came running after me in the parking lot.

I sometimes wonder about the backstory of the Samaritan

in Jesus' parable. Had he himself once been the victim of a brutal crime? Perhaps not, but he certainly knew the sting of rejection. It's no accident that Jesus used a Samaritan in the story. Samaritans were hated by the Jews and considered enemies. This man would have known what it felt like to be despised, tossed aside, and ignored. Perhaps that's why he couldn't just walk by. Instead of seeing only costly inconvenience in a heap of bloodied flesh, the Samaritan saw a physical representation of how he had been treated all his life. He saw more than what was readily visible. He saw a person . . . a neighbor.

When I read the story of the good Samaritan, it's hard to understand the lack of action by the priest and the Levite. How could they justify passing by the man in need? How could they be so heartless? But perhaps it wasn't cruelty that made them unwilling to act. Maybe they just didn't know what to do.

There were plenty of people at Trader Joe's that day who could have stopped staring and instead offered assistance to our family. Those who gave us a wide berth could have chosen instead to smile and make eye contact to let me know they understood and that I was doing fine. The stares that felt like judgment didn't come from evil people; they came from those who didn't understand. Those who avoided us may have simply been afraid of getting it wrong—of saying words that hurt instead of helped—so the road of neutrality seemed safest. Perhaps they followed the priest and the Levite to the other side of the road and assured themselves that doing nothing was the loving response simply because they didn't know what else to do.

I was in eighth grade when I first learned, with heartbreaking clarity, the true atrocities of the Holocaust. I vividly remember sitting in the second row of desks in social studies class while we watched a documentary about Hitler's systematic murder of six million Jews. I'd learned bits and pieces about it before, but this was the most thorough, visual, and detailed account I'd ever encountered. My classmates shifted uncomfortably in their seats, a few gasped every now and then, but most just sat as still and heavy as stones. As I watched, tears streamed down my face until the credits rolled, and I excused myself to the restroom.

Later, I learned about Elie Wiesel, a Romanian-born author, professor, and Holocaust survivor. Wiesel wasn't much older than my eighth-grade self when he and his family were sent to Auschwitz, where his mother and younger sister were murdered. He and his father were later sent to the concentration camp at Buchenwald. He survived, but his father did not. Wiesel subsequently dedicated his life to speaking out against dehumanization in all its forms and sharing his own story as a guide to compassion, hope, and humanity. In a 1986 interview with US News & World Report, Wiesel spoke these sobering words:

> The opposite of love is not hate, it's indifference. The opposite of art is not ugliness, it's indifference. The opposite of faith is not heresy, it's indifference. And the opposite of life is not death, it's indifference. Because of indifference, one dies before one actually dies. To be in the window and

watch people being sent to concentration camps or being attacked in the street and do nothing, that's being dead.

We see this truth reflected so clearly in the story of the good Samaritan. Only one passerby was credited with loving his neighbor—the other two are simply known for their indifference. If confronted, I wonder if the priest or Levite would protest, "We didn't do anything wrong! We didn't beat and rob the man. We were simply minding our own business. We didn't know what to do." And yet, indifference is the unloving behavior.

If indifference is the disease, empathy is the antidote. Empathy propels us beyond our apathy and fears. Empathy guides us out of indifference and into the messy, hard, heartbreaking, personal lives of the people around us. Empathy reminds us, "We are interdependent. Each of us depends on the well-being of the whole."[1] We cannot love our neighbor well until we embrace empathy.

My favorite feel-good movie is the 1998 rom-com *You've Got Mail*. I like to watch it each autumn with a mug of hot cider while I think about bouquets of freshly sharpened pencils and the smell of Scotch tape. One of my favorite exchanges between the main characters, Joe and Kathleen—played by Tom Hanks and Meg Ryan—happens in her apartment. He has just put her tiny bookstore out of business and wants her forgiveness. He tries reasoning that it wasn't personal—it was business.

"What is that supposed to mean?" Kathleen asks. "I am so sick of that. All that means is that it wasn't personal to *you*. But it was personal to me. It's personal to a lot of people. And what's so wrong with being personal, anyway? Whatever else anything is, it ought to begin by being personal."[2]

I'm certain the good Samaritan would have agreed. Empathy begins by being personal, by seeing the individual behind the situation. By checking on the normally bright-eyed and interested child who is suddenly sullen and distracted at school, by digging deeper to ask how policies or laws we support or vote for actually impact the daily lives of our neighbors near and far, by pausing regularly to look inward and honestly reflect on how the way we move through life impacts the people around us. It's the key to how we love our neighbors in a world marked by fear and division.

I sometimes wonder what might have happened to the man the Samaritan helped. Did he go home and tell his friends that they'd been wrong all along about the Samaritans? Did he commit his life to treating others with the same love and care he had received? Did he become a catalyst for peace between Samaritans and Jews? We don't know, and it's just a parable after all. But maybe it could be more than that. Maybe it could be an invitation to write the next chapter of the story ourselves. We're called to love our neighbors as ourselves—to love as we ourselves have been loved by our heavenly Father. We're called to resist the pull of indifference by reaching for empathy. The rest of the story is yet to be written; the pen is in our hands, and tomorrow is a blank page.

Whatever we do, let's begin by being personal.

# WE ALL FALL DOWN

The dream of safety dies hard.
JAMES BALDWIN, *IF BEALE STREET COULD TALK*

**M**areto was about eight months old when he got extremely sick in the late-night hours. Before tucking into bed ourselves, John and I heard a faint cry from Mareto's room and went to check on him. He was whimpering and surrounded by vomit. I gently lifted him out of the mess and carried him to the bathroom for a sponge bath. He felt too warm, so I grabbed the digital thermometer to check his temperature. At the quiet beep-beep, I looked down to see 104.5° flashing back at me. Alarmed, I called to John, who was cleaning out the crib. We packed the diaper bag and drove to the emergency room.

While we waited, I was a little worried—as most first-time mothers are when their baby spikes a fever—but still relatively calm. I held my son against my chest and adjusted the blanket I'd swaddled him in. After nurses took his vitals, asked us the same questions over and over and over, ushered us into a semi-private room, and we waited even longer, the doctor finally arrived. It was nearly 1:00 a.m., and everyone was tired.

The doctor briefly examined Mareto and then quickly signed the discharge papers with his diagnosis: teething. I wish I were joking, but this man who had completed years of medical school and had been practicing medicine for several more years, actually told us that many babies run a fever when they teethe. We were new parents and didn't know that babies absolutely do not run fevers in excess of 104° when teething. We didn't know that we should ask to see someone else. We didn't know anything except that we felt foolish for coming to the emergency room for teething.

We sheepishly thanked the doctor and collected our things. Mareto had been quiet and sleepy throughout, and for that I was grateful, but not surprised. Mareto was a quiet baby, and his cries always had a purpose: either he wanted food or to be held. Once those needs were met, he was quiet and content. I wrapped him in a blanket and gathered him to my chest.

As we made our way around the circular hallway that led back to the waiting room and the exit, I could hear another baby crying. Well, *shrieking* might be a better description. The more we walked, the louder the cries became. Just before we reached the exit, I glanced through the open door of an exam room. Two young parents stood several steps away from a hospital bed while a team of doctors and nurses hovered over a very small baby who was protesting with all its might. The mother's hands covered her mouth, and her face was twisted in agony. The father's arm was around her waist, his concerned gaze fixed on the tiny person screaming and flailing. They stood motionless.

I turned away and tried to swallow the lump in my throat. I gave John a look that said, *I am so relieved we aren't the family in the room with the screaming baby.*

"I know," he said. "That was so sad."

On the way home, I couldn't get the image of that mother out of my mind. I kept wondering how she could just stand there watching while her baby thrashed in pain and screamed out in fear. *I wouldn't be able to do that,* I thought. *Someone would have to physically hold me back to keep me from that bed. I would have been holding my baby, comforting him.* I made a mental list of all the ways I would have acted differently in that situation because I loved my son too much to just stand by and watch him hurt. I looked back at Mareto, asleep in his car seat, and smiled at his chubby cheeks, reassuring myself that I didn't need to think about that heart-wrenching scene anymore. My baby was fine—just teething.

The next morning we woke after too few hours of sleep, and I tried to feed Mareto. But he wasn't interested in the bottle, and his eyes were glassy. I noticed his lips seemed awfully dry and a thin dusting of white outlined his mouth. I pressed my hand against his face and immediately drew it back, stunned at the heat radiating off his head. John went for the thermometer, and I tried to coax the bottle into Mareto's mouth once more. A few more moments, a few short beeps, and then . . . panic. The digital number flashing back at us this time was 105.9°.

I gasped and fumbled for my cell phone. My hands shook as I dialed the number for the pediatrician. The nurse listened intently and then put me on hold while she spoke with the doctor. She came back with a single command: "Go to the emergency room. Now!"

I cried silently as I grabbed the diaper bag and hurriedly tied my shoelaces. Just before we pulled out of the driveway, my phone rang—it was the nurse calling with more instructions. "Pack him with ice!" she instructed, in a tone that fell short of professional calm. John ran back inside and came out with a few bags of frozen peas. I tucked them under Mareto's arms while John peeled out of the cul-de-sac and onto the highway. Less than fifteen minutes later, we were back in the same ER we'd left less than eight hours earlier. And within an hour, we were living out the wrenching scene I'd tried to shake from my mind the night before.

They made eleven attempts to find a vein. Eleven times a stranger poked a needle into my baby boy while he screamed. Several nurses, including a NICU nurse, couldn't get the IV into Mareto. He was too dehydrated, too small, and too upset. He screamed, and I cried next to him, trying to soothe the panic I saw building in his eyes. A team of nurses surrounded his hospital bed, and I tried to reach out to touch him—to let him know I hadn't left and I never would. But the nurses needed me to stand back and let them work. I was in the way. In that moment, the most loving thing I could do for my son was to temporarily let him go.

In the intervals between needles, I held Mareto's feverish

body close to mine and sang softly into his ear. *Let him rest!* I thought whenever the nurses returned to try again. *Please just let him be!* But this was an emergency, and no one could rest until he was okay. So I laid him on the bed once more and stepped away, watching silently with my hands over my mouth, my face contorted. John wrapped an arm around me and watched intently. After the eleventh attempt, the medical team gave up and transferred us to a different hospital.

I rode in the back of the ambulance with Mareto. He was strapped into a car seat that was strapped onto a gurney, and I was on the bench—one hand on the diaper bag, the other holding tightly to my son. I was struggling to process the quick shift in events. One moment we'd been having a quiet evening at home, the next we were driving to the emergency room. One moment we were going to sleep with a teething baby, the next we were packing him with ice and racing to the hospital. One moment I was turning my face from a frightened mother with a screaming child, and the next I was standing precisely where she had been, helplessly watching a team of nurses and doctors hover over my son.

Nearly twenty-four hours later and at a new hospital, we found success. An IV had been placed, tests had been run, and we got some fluid into our extremely dehydrated little boy. When the results came back, I had to swallow my anger at the first doctor. Of course Mareto wasn't teething—he had a dangerous kidney infection. Medications lowered his critically high fever, the IV fluids rehydrated his small body, and a series of injected antibiotics over the course of the next few days got rid of the infection. Within a week, he was back to his normal, chubby, babbling self. But I've never forgotten that other baby and the parents who stood helplessly watching. I've never forgotten how I closed my eyes to their pain and comforted myself with the thought that it wasn't me, wasn't my child, and wouldn't be our story. And even if it ever was, that I would do it differently . . . better.

Our experiences over that twenty-four hours taught me two things: First, no one is immune to tragedy. And second, we actually have no idea what we'll do when our turn comes. Everything we think will be the "right" way to handle a crisis gets turned upside down, and we have to do things we never expected or thought we'd ever do. These were lessons that came back to me when a hurricane hit Texas.

❧

In August 2017, Hurricane Harvey dumped more than forty inches of rain over a four-day period and caused unprecedented flooding in Southeast Texas. The Houston metro area was especially hard hit, with nearly a third of the city under water, the weight of which caused the city to temporarily sink two centimeters.[1] In the aftermath, countless people far from Texas wondered aloud and online why the residents of Houston didn't evacuate ahead of the storm. Speculation and criticism ran rampant while quick Twitter fingers typed out what *they* would have done in a brief 140 characters. Perhaps they did not realize—or did not care—that their comments only heaped additional anguish on already suffering neighbors.

But there, in the midst of all those opinions, was a group of people who saw no room for such judgment, only the need for compassion. They were called the Cajun Navy, a collection of volunteers from Louisiana who hitched their boats to their trucks and showed up in Texas ready to help. One member of this makeshift rescue squad described how his own home had flooded during Hurricane Katrina twelve years earlier. "I lost all kinds of things," he said. When he heard about the flooding in Houston, he decided: "I'm not going to work. I'm going to head that way and meet up with somebody and do what I can do."[2] This man had no judgment for the residents of Houston because he had stood in floodwaters himself, and now he was able to offer compassion and help to pull others from similar waters.

The self-righteous idea that we've somehow set up our lives in ways that protect us from certain kinds of crises, implying that those who are experiencing said crises have not, is what keeps many of us from entering into the painful places in another person's life, grabbing their hands with zero judgment, and offering nothing but love, grace, and presence. It's what keeps us from realizing, as chaos unfolds for another, *It could be me, and I have no idea why it isn't this time.*

Finding ourselves neck-deep in crisis might be the very thing it takes to remind us that we're all just a breath away from tragedy. Our own pain might be the one thing that causes us to stop closing our eyes to the mother in the exam room, turning our faces from the man lying under the bridge, and turning off the news of children dying in detention centers. It's easy to ignore or judge suffering when we naïvely assume it will never be us. But just as the nursery rhyme says, "Ashes, ashes, we all fall down."

I struggle a bit with generalized anxiety. I remain hyper-vigilant at all times to make sure my kids are okay, our home remains standing, and the dog doesn't keel over dead. Hypervigilance is the voice within that urges me to double-check the smoke detectors and deadbolts. It's the voice that tells the kids, "No food in bed." Not because they've already brushed their teeth, or they might get crumbs in the sheets, attracting ants or mice . . . no. It's the fear that they might choke on a bite of food, and I'd never know until I found them unconscious, or worse, the next morning.

I put a lot of time and effort into seeking out safety in every possible corner of life. I google things such as "safest places to live in the United States" and then compare everything from crime statistics and city size to weather—yes, *weather.* Is that location smack-dab in the middle of Tornado Alley? Is it known for earthquakes or hurricanes or flash floods? What about wildfires?

We currently live in an area that checks a lot of my safety boxes. The weather is usually mild, the crime rate is low, and the population quite small. Our block is quiet, and close friends live right across the street. My husband has a steady job, and I can walk to the closest hospital if needed. There are two cars in our driveway, food in the cupboards, shoes and warm coats in the closets, and a card in my wallet that gets us healthcare and medicine as needed.

There is some comfort in these things that provides safety, but I also see them for what they really are: illusions. The truth is, no amount of hypervigilance can make my life untouchable. I can't be rich enough to buy myself a pain-free life, I can't be pretty enough to charm my way out of suffering, and I certainly can't be good enough to avoid it. Because crisis can, and does, knock on every door. Which might be part of why John and I love watching the Canadian sitcom *Schitt's Creek*.

*Schitt's Creek* tells the hilarious riches-to-rags story of a family who loses everything when their business manager defrauds them. The show's pilot episode opens with the ringing of a doorbell in an otherwise silent and serene mansion. A group of government officials is waiting on the porch to repossess the house and its contents. A scream rings out, and then we see the parents, Johnny and Moira, and their two adult children, David and Alexis, running through the house, trying to stuff as many of their possessions as they can into bags. There is shouting and chaos one minute, and the next we see the family of four sitting shell-shocked on a couch as they listen to their lawyer explain that they have lost everything. The rest of the show follows them as they move into a motel in the tiny town of Schitt's Creek and learn how to start over from scratch. It's funny, endearing, and sometimes hits a little too close to home when it holds up a sort of funhouse mirror to our own tendencies toward pride and the illusion of safety.

As exaggerated as the characters are, I can't help but relate as they struggle to grasp the harsh realities of their unexpected new life. My friends and I know only too well what that's like. Such as being pregnant one day and leaving the maternity ward with empty arms the next. Or when, in the span of twelve months, my best friend Rachel was diagnosed with colon cancer, her sister was diagnosed with breast cancer, her mother's cancer returned, her mother passed away, and then her husband's job transferred them to another state. Even if we are billionaires with giant mansions who can jet off to Cabo for the weekend, life rips the rug out from under all of us at some point, and we rarely see it coming.

Job is perhaps the closest equivalent the ancient world had to a jet-setting, mansion-residing billionaire. Considered the "greatest of all the people of the east," he had "7,000 sheep, 3,000 camels, 500 yoke of oxen, and 500 female donkeys, and very many servants" (Job 1:3). And if that weren't enough to make him great, it turns out he was also virtually sinless. God himself described Job as "a blameless and upright man, who fears God and turns away from evil" (Job 1:8). This was a man of integrity and faith and goodness. He worked hard and lived well and had earned his great fortune. Life was good, as was Job. He raised ten healthy children, built homes and barns and fences, and honored God in all he did. And then, in the space of one day, he lost it all.

One servant came to tell him that raiding Sabeans had taken the oxen and donkeys and killed the servants who cared for them. Before he could finish his report, another servant ran up to tell Job that fire fell from heaven and burned up all the sheep and the servants who cared for them. And before that message was complete, still another servant rushed in to inform Job that raiding Chaldeans had taken the camels and killed the attending servants. True to form, yet another servant rushed in to announce that the house in which his ten children were feasting had collapsed and killed them all. One moment Job's life was wonderful, and the next it was shattered. And just when we might be tempted to say, "Well, at least Job still had his health," this blameless and upright man was struck with a disease that caused "loathsome sores from the sole of his foot to the crown of his head" (Job 2:7).

Some who know the rest of Job's story might argue that we really can earn our way to a carefree life because, by the end of the book, we learn that Job was healed, all of his wealth was restored to him, and he went on to have more children and even more prosperity. But I would argue that if we could, then surely John the Baptist wouldn't have been beheaded, the apostle Paul would have been cured of the thorn in his side, and Stephen wouldn't have been stoned to death.

I think the story of Job illustrates a much different truth. Perhaps what it's really telling us is that we can be good, wise, and faithful and still lose everything. That life is hard, but God is still good. That the "happy ending" to Job's story is one that points us to the hope of heaven and the treasure that awaits us there, in spite of our suffering here on Earth.

Even if we never experience suffering and loss to the degree Job did, none of us can avoid heartbreak forever. We're all just one phone call, one knock at the front door, one storm, one regrettable decision away from the worst day of our lives. And if we're not currently sitting in the wreckage of what used to be a peaceful life, we are just an arm's reach away from someone who is. The temptation to turn our faces can be strong. After all, we don't want to be reminded of the fragility of our own happy existence. We want to believe that if we work hard enough and live well enough, we can protect ourselves and our loved ones from disaster. The falling apart? That's what happens to someone else.

It's amazing how many people buy into the illusion of the "self-made" man or woman—of working hard enough and being good enough to earn or create an untouchable life. I have long been critical of the prosperity gospel—the idea that if you have enough faith, God will bless you with material wealth and an easy life. And yet, how many times have I looked at the suffering of my neighbor and thought, *That will never be me*? How many times have I rearranged some corner of my life for safety? How many times have I googled safeguards against crime, double-checked the smoke detectors, reached for the Dave Ramsey DVDs, and read yet another parenting book in a vain effort to disaster-proof my life?

I may be a slow learner, but pain is an effective teacher. While we'd never ask for calamity, it is the moments of crisis that shape our hearts, strengthen our resolve, fine-tune our perspective, and grow our empathy for others. If empathy is the ability to walk a mile in someone else's shoes, doing so becomes far easier when we look down to see the scuffed toes, fraying laces, and holes in the soles of our own sneakers. When our own shoes are ragged and worn, we're no longer reluctant to take them for a walk down our neighbor's muddy path.

The harsh reality is that it's just not possible to live a life void of suffering. And knowing that we all fall down should make us a little more gracious, and a little more generous, and a little gentler when those around us do. It should make us not just willing but eager to sit with our suffering neighbor and offer any comfort possible, knowing that one day we may need them to do the same with us. Pride is the devil on my shoulder, whispering in my ear, "This will never be you." And if it ever was, I convince myself I'd do it differently. Better. But empathy whispers to my heart, "This could be me. How can I love today?"

# BLIND SPOTS

I would not have you descend into your own dream. I would have you be a conscious citizen of this terrible and beautiful world.

TA-NEHISI COATES, *BETWEEN THE WORLD AND ME*

In the summer of 1995, my family drove from San Diego, California, to our new home in Fairfax County, Virginia. It was on this cross-country drive that I memorized every song from my mom's Carole King album, learned that the Midwest is unbelievably flat, and discovered the canvas top to my dad's Mustang convertible had a few holes in it as torrential rain leaked through and my sister caught the downpour with her shoe. It was also the summer I learned about blind spots.

By the time we finally pulled up to our new home on Cordwood Court, I'd heard my dad say two things numerous times and in various ranges of volume, "Get out of my blind spot!" and "I've got to get out of this guy's blind spot!" as cars passed us or we passed them on the highway. When we were still somewhere out West, maybe passing through Nevada, my mom went to change lanes and hit a car next to her. It wasn't a bad accident—no one was hurt and the dents on the cars weren't terrible—but I heard over and over again how the car next to her had been in her blind spot. At some point I finally asked my dad what a blind spot was.

He pointed out the tricky spots every vehicle has that make it difficult for the driver to see another car in the side or rearview mirrors. "That's why," he told me, "you have to also turn your head and look for things in your blind spot before you change lanes. You have to look for things that don't appear to be there at first glance."

We all have blind spots—things we don't see that are nevertheless there. Our blindness to them might stem from ignorance, lack of awareness, or prejudice. Whether realized or not, blind spots arise whenever a voice within convinces us, *If it's not happening to me, it's not happening.* When we believe this, we miss out on an opportunity to love those among us who are hurting and maybe even set ourselves on a collision course to be the cause of their pain.

I was nineteen years old and a sophomore in college when I met John. We quickly connected, started dating, and were engaged less than a year later. At the time, I wasn't looking for a serious relationship, let alone marriage. I'd planned on

remaining single and just "playing the field," as my grand-
mother would say, while I finished college and figured out
what I wanted to do with the rest of my life. But then I met
John, and I fell hard. He was kind, handsome, easy to talk
to, funny, and tall. And, importantly, he liked me. I mean,
he really liked me for who I was deep down. He thought the
things I hated about myself (my voice and extremely sensitive
nature) were endearing. He wanted to hear about what I
found interesting. Finding love was ridiculously easy for me.

A few months after our engagement, I sat cross-legged
on the floor of my college Baptist Student Union. I wasn't a
Baptist, but the year before I had been looking for a campus
Bible study, and these girls had enthusiastically welcomed
me. So there I sat on a Tuesday evening, surrounded by
friends and a few girls I didn't know. We listened as different
people shared things that were coming up in their week or
troubles they were facing. Occasionally someone would offer
helpful advice, or we would stop to pray about something as
a group. Then a girl I didn't know began to share.

I can still picture her sitting on the arm of an old, refur-
bished armchair. She was tall and slender with long black
hair and an olive complexion. She was gorgeous. I don't
remember what prompted it, but she was expressing her
frustration with the lack of eligible males on campus. She
ended with a defeated, "Why is it so hard to find a nice guy
who wants to have more than a fling?"

Sitting here now, I can think of numerous responses I
wish I had given—silence paired with a listening ear being
top of the list. I wish I'd told her I was sorry. I wish I'd gotten to know her better and been able to support her as she

worked through her feelings of disappointment and rejection. Maybe I should have hugged her and just agreed that a lot of college guys don't treat their female peers with the respect they deserve. So what did I actually do, you ask? Ugh.

I chuckled smugly, looked down at the diamond sparkling on my left hand, and waved it at her as I said, "It's not *that* hard."

Yes. That was my response. My arrogant, unsympathetic, callous response. It wasn't hard for *me* to find love. Therefore, it couldn't really be that hard.

I have a counselor today who would call that an "empathic failure." To say the least! I felt a twinge of conviction later in the evening when I returned to my apartment. I remember thinking that, while I hadn't meant to be rude, it probably wasn't the kindest response. It wasn't until several years later, when John and I were suffering through infertility, that I really understood just how cruel I'd actually been.

The tables were turned, and now I was the one who had to listen to others share that it really wasn't "*that* hard" to get pregnant. I found myself avoiding certain social situations and conversations because I just couldn't face another person telling me to relax and it would happen, or try a vitamin or oils, or just quit trying, or—cringe—joke about taking a swig from the water fountain at church, since a baby boom seemed to be happening.

It wasn't hard for them. Infertility wasn't happening to them. They weren't grieving the crushing loss of a dream month after month. They weren't crying in the bathroom during baby showers. They weren't fielding phone calls from reproduction specialists with depressing news. It had been easy for them, so in their minds, pregnancy and having children was just . . . easy.

"Centering" is what happens when we consider our own experiences to be universal, and it's one of the biggest roadblocks to empathy. Centering our experience creates a blind spot that makes it impossible to see other people and the truth of their experiences. It's a dynamic brilliantly illustrated in a cartoon I saw recently.

Two eagles are sitting in lounge chairs sipping tea.

"Do you think the owl is a predator?" asks one eagle.

"Of course not," the other eagle responds, "he's never bothered me!"

"Exactly," the first eagle says. "I don't know what that silly mouse was talking about."

When we center our own experiences and consider them normative, we become blind to the pain, injustice, suffering, and discrimination experienced by others.

Centering makes the experiences of others seem far away, uncommon, and not part of our world. So when someone different from us crosses our path and says, "Hey, I'm in pain here," our instinct is to minimize it, explain it away, or assume it's an isolated incident. Instead of setting ourselves aside and viewing life through the eyes and pain of another, we point to our own experiences as Exhibit A for why this person's experience can't possibly be true. That's a blind spot.

If we want to love our neighbor well, we need to check our blind spots.

In October 2017, investigative reporters Jodi Kantor and Megan Twohey published a piece in the *New York Times* titled "Harvey Weinstein Paid Off Sexual Harassment Accusers for Decades." The bombshell article detailed an extensive history of sexual assault and harassment allegations against the powerful movie mogul. Within the week, another investigative reporter, Ronan Farrow, published an explosive exposé in *The New Yorker* titled "From Aggressive Overtures to Sexual Assault: Harvey Weinstein's Accusers Tell Their Stories." By the next week, the phrase "Me Too," first coined over a decade earlier by activist Tarana Burke, had reemerged as a hashtag and was taking social media by storm. The #MeToo movement against sexual assault and sexual harassment went on to topple the careers of other powerful men once considered untouchable.

As the movement found its footing, I read quotes from male actors who expressed shock at the experiences their female counterparts described. "I never saw Weinstein do anything like this," said one. "He always treated me with respect," said another.

When I first told John about some of my own experiences—the times I'd been followed to my car, catcalled, or had my appearance commented on by strangers while with my children—he was shocked too. He can walk down the street, through a parking garage, and to the restroom in a restaurant in peace. He hasn't had to master the art of being dismissive and firm enough to end an unwanted interaction but kind enough not to incite anger and violence.

My husband had a blind spot, but he wasn't committed to it. Over the years of our marriage, he has changed and grown. He listens when I share my experiences, holds my hand in counseling sessions, and pays attention to what the world is like for me, for our daughter, and for other women. Because he loves me and shares his life with me, because he respects me and listens to my voice, because he values my experience and believes me when I share it, his perspective on life has expanded, and he has one less blind spot.

If we want to be intentional about checking our blind spots, we need to look at why they exist, how they persist, and how we can keep from running others off the road as we barrel through life full speed ahead.

When I was in college, money was tight. Even so, I knew I had it better than many of my peers. My parents paid for my tuition, books, rent, and grocery bills, so it was just spending money that was my responsibility. If I wanted to go out to dinner with friends, buy new shoes, or go to the movies, that came from my own wallet.

I had a variety of part-time jobs throughout college, mostly as a waitress or retail clerk, but I didn't work many hours and the wages weren't exactly high. In my final year of school, nearly all the money from my paychecks went to payments for my soon-to-be husband's wedding band. Because my parents were covering all my living expenses, that wasn't a big deal. I knew I could do without new clothes, movies, and dining out. But three other friends were also getting married that summer, and with weddings come expenses.

One friend planned a party to celebrate her upcoming

nuptials and chose an extremely swanky downtown restaurant as the location for this event. It was important that I show up, but as the day grew closer, I knew I'd have no more than twenty dollars to spend that evening. *No problem,* I thought, *I can make twenty dollars go a long way for myself.* That was, until I glanced at the menu and saw that a simple side salad cost nearly fifteen dollars. I frantically read every line of the menu, looking for the least expensive thing offered. When the waiter got to me, I half whispered my order, "I'll have water with lemon and a side salad, please." As he continued to look at me, waiting for the rest of my order, my cheeks flushed and I stared back, silently begging him not to draw any attention to me. It took a moment, but I saw a look of understanding pass over his face, and he nodded before taking my menu and moving on.

I went back to laughing with my friends before a few cheese platters began to appear on the table. Someone had ordered them "for the group," and I panicked. *Are we splitting the cost of the appetizers?* I didn't know, so I didn't take a single bite for fear that I would be expected to chip in. Soon, the dinner plates were delivered. Everyone had ordered things like steak and salmon and roast chicken—actual meals. When my salad was placed in front of me, I looked down to see a small pile of lettuce (I'm sure it was fancy lettuce, but still, it was just lettuce to me), a few candied pecans, and a drizzle of dressing. I glanced up to see a few of my friends looking at my plate in confusion. Embarrassed, I refused to make eye contact and tucked into my salad. To my great relief, no one said a word about my meal, and I was not asked to contribute to the cost of the appetizers. I was able to pay my share of the check and had enough money left over to leave a tip.

At the time, I was a little resentful that no thought had been given to the possibility that not everyone could afford the cost of the evening. I went home after the dinner, well before the celebrations were over, because I couldn't afford to attend the rest of the events. My friend was a little hurt that I left early, but I didn't know how to tell her I was out of money without feeling like I was asking her to cover my costs. It was an awkward experience at the time, but one for which I've been extremely grateful in the years since.

Before that evening, I'd never really had to worry too much about money. In fact, I could easily have been the one choosing an expensive restaurant, clueless that someone I had invited might not be able to afford it. But in the years since, I've had to decline numerous invitations for lack of funds. As a result, I've learned that insufficient funds is nothing to be ashamed of. It's helped me to be more aware and considerate of those around me, because I don't assume everyone has the same financial resources I do. And it also helps to be able to laugh about it, which John and I do every time we watch a rerun of a highly relatable episode of *Friends* titled, "The One with Five Steaks and an Eggplant."

In this episode, Chandler is planning Ross's upcoming birthday party, and his plans include a gift, a cake, and a concert. Meanwhile, Monica gets a promotion at work and comes home eager to celebrate, so she recommends everyone go out for a fancy dinner. Rachel, Joey, and Phoebe realize they can't afford to pay their portion of Ross's birthday celebration *and* this fancy dinner, so they end up doing what I did in college—ordering the least expensive things on the menu. My favorite line is when the waiter (who is not as perceptive as mine was) responds to Rachel ordering a side salad by asking, "And what will that be on the side of?" The whole dinner is tense and awkward as Chandler, Monica, and Ross continue on throughout the evening oblivious to how stressed and uncomfortable the other three are.

Chandler, Monica, and Ross love their friends, and they aren't really doing anything wrong. They simply have a blind spot. When Phoebe finally speaks up and lets them know how hard it is to pay for things they take for granted, Ross says, "Well, I guess I just never think of money as an issue." To which Rachel responds, "That's cause you have it."[1]

We miss a lot when we center our experiences by assuming they are the norm. When someone shares their reality and we find ourselves scratching our heads and unable to understand, we can choose our response. Instead of minimizing their experience or defending our own, we could acknowledge that perhaps we don't see the full picture. Perhaps we have a blind spot.

＊

In my last semester of college, something strange began happening to me—whenever I got cold, I developed a very itchy rash. It usually began on the insides of my wrists and quickly spread to my forearms and often popped up on my feet before creeping up my legs. It drove me absolutely nuts as I struggled to sit through class or in the library without scratching madly at my red, swollen skin. The first couple of times, I assumed I had brushed up against someone wearing a Bath and Body Works lotion, to which I am highly allergic (which made high school tricky since it was the go-to lotion for nearly every girl there). But it kept happening over several weeks and often when I was alone. It seemed to come out of nowhere, drive me nuts, then fade away—sometimes all within an hour or two.

One evening I was at my in-laws' home for dinner when the rash began to develop on my feet and then spread rapidly to my legs. I excused myself and went to the bathroom to put a cold cloth on them to relieve the itching. When my mother-in-law, a nurse, came to check on me and saw the angry red welts covering my legs, she exclaimed, "Oh, my goodness! You need to see a doctor!" She found a tube of anti-itch cream to help me through the evening, and the welts were gone by the next day. I went back to my regular schedule of class, studying, and trying to graduate in the next few weeks.

John and I had only been married a few months and, because I was in my last semester of school, we lived apart during the week. Our apartment and John's job were a four-hour drive from my college. During the week, I stayed with my parents, who lived thirty minutes from school, and on the weekends, I drove home to our newlywed apartment. I was no longer covered under my parents' medical insurance but had not yet selected a general practitioner under my new insurance. I wanted to wait until I had graduated and permanently moved to our new city to find a doctor, so I tried to ignore the rash while I powered through until graduation.

When the time finally came, I asked around for doctor recommendations and found myself sitting in the office of a small country doctor. My skin was clear at the time, but I wasn't worried about it. In fact, I was relieved to be able to talk to someone and hopefully get some answers. After the physician introduced himself, I explained my problem. He looked a little skeptical and said, "Okay, well let's see that rash." As he turned to wash his hands, I explained that I didn't currently have the rash. He looked at me over the rims of his glasses and said in a patronizing tone, "Well, that's convenient." I was dumbfounded and didn't know what to say. "You know what they say," he continued, "the squeaky wheel gets the grease. But your wheel isn't squeaking."

I stared back at him, confused, until it hit me that he didn't believe me. He couldn't see the rash; therefore, it wasn't happening to me. I left the office minutes later and found a new doctor.

Thankfully, the next physician took the time to listen (and I brought along pictures of my hives). He asked good questions, and together we identified a pattern. I only got the hives when I was cold or touched something very cold, and the only thing that made them go away was a warm shower. Finally, we found the answer: *cold urticaria*. I was literally allergic to being cold. I left his office armed with a pack of antihistamines and relieved to have been heard, believed, and helped.

Blind spots can cause real damage to hurting people. I know that, and yet I have to wonder how often I respond to others as the first doctor did to me. What is my first reaction when I'm confronted with a problem I can't initially see? Is it to look deeper, listen more intently, and try to understand? Or is it to doubt and dismiss?

When I read the Gospels, I am struck by how many of the people Jesus interacted with came from the margins. These were the people who hovered nearby, in trees, outside the temple, and near the city gates—each one a blind spot for the mainstream men and women who moved through life largely unaffected by them. But Jesus had no blind spots. He saw each marginalized, overlooked person and often praised them as examples of faith. These were people worth listening to and stopping for.

When parents of sick children ran to him in fear, he didn't dismiss them—he helped. When a despised tax collector invited him to dinner, Jesus ate with him. When the blind asked for healing, he gave them sight. On page after page, I see Jesus stop, recognize, and validate the people others routinely relegated to the sidelines. He invites us to do the same.

We can't love neighbors who reside in our blind spots. But if we practice paying attention, if we're diligent about looking to see what might be hidden in plain sight, we will begin to see as Jesus sees. We need to look deeper when we encounter people and experiences that don't initially make sense to us. We need to believe others when they tell us about their perspectives or pain, and we need to seek to understand them when we don't. We can start by decentering ourselves so we can see others through the eyes of Christ. When we do that, we will be surprised to see how many neighbors have been waiting to be seen.

# FOUR

# BORN FOR OTHERS

If we have no peace, it is because we have forgotten that
we belong to each other.
MOTHER TERESA

L ast December I found myself sitting at a folding table in
the recreation room of a local nursing home, unloading
boxes of colored pencils and bottles of nail polish. I was
nervous and hesitant. *Is this ridiculous?* Maybe. I arranged
the bottles by color—a few bright, a few dark, and a few
neutrals. I lined up the clippers and nail files and adjusted
them a few times because nerves make me a bit obsessive
that way. I scattered the colored pencils around the table and
tore pages from an adult coloring book. The entire time my
inner voice was telling me, *This is dumb. No one is going to
enjoy these activities, Lauren.* But I didn't know what else
to do, so I stuck with my plan.

My friend Lynn visits this nursing home the first and third Thursdays of the month and had invited me to join her. When she arrives, she always greets everyone with a warm smile and a bright, "Good morning!" Beginning promptly at 9:30 a.m., she pulls out the piano bench, opens her music book or hymnal, and plays songs she thinks the residents will enjoy. It's mostly old hymns, Broadway tunes, and big band hits, then she closes with "Jesus Loves Me" no later than 10:25 a.m. Bingo starts at 10:30 a.m., and you don't interfere with bingo.

As usual, a gentleman named Philip was the first to arrive, wearing the same hat he'd worn last time we came—a black baseball cap with a cross and "John 14:6" embroidered above the bill. As Lynn wheeled him through the doors, I noticed his wrist was in a splint. I invited him to sit next to me at the table and offered him a coloring sheet and some pencils. Philip looked through the sheets and told me about a woman in a room down the hall from his who loved to color but was still sleeping. He asked if he could take some of the coloring sheets back to her room as a gift. "She'll love these," he said with a smile. I asked if he wanted to color, but he was already watching Lynn and listening to the music, so I didn't push it.

I grabbed a pencil and coloring sheet to give my hands something to do and turned back to see Philip watching me, so I asked him what had happened to his hand. "It's paralyzed," he told me. "I had a stroke, and my entire left side from the arm down is paralyzed." He looked back at Lynn, and it was clear he was done talking for a bit. We sat together quietly as Lynn continued to play hymns. Philip watched her intently and exclaimed between songs that she was the most talented musician he'd ever heard.

A few minutes later, a woman shuffled her wheelchair over to the end of the table next to Philip. I smiled and said good morning, but she stared right past me to Philip, who set a few pencils and a coloring sheet in front of her. She grabbed his arm, and he put a blue pencil in her hand. Then she looked down and began to lightly scribble inside the block letters that spelled out LOVE.

As I watched her coloring her sheet, I noticed her bright red nail polish was badly chipped and the ends of her nails were broken at jagged edges. I asked if she might like me to paint her nails and gestured toward my bag of supplies. She stared back at me silently.

As I sat there awkwardly wondering what to do next, she lifted her hands and looked at her nails, then back up at me. I took that as a sign that she wanted her nails painted and wheeled my stool over to her. She wasn't able to communicate verbally, and I didn't know her well enough to understand any other ways she might have been trying to communicate. So I picked a color of polish that matched her pants and apologized for not being a professional.

I gently removed the remnants of red polish from her nails, clipped the broken edges, and filed them down to a smooth, rounded finish. She couldn't support the weight of her hand and wouldn't set it on the table, so I went about my task one-handed—my right hand grabbing cotton balls and the bottle of polish, my left hand cupping hers and holding it up. I worked quickly as Lynn continued to sere-nade us all. When the first set of nails were finished, Philip piped up, "Oh, those are beautiful!"

As I started on the woman's other hand, Lynn began to play the old gospel song "In the Garden." Suddenly a loud voice rang out—the woman was trying to sing along. Her mouth could no longer form the words, but she was belting out a hum as she followed the melody. I looked at her face and knew—this was her song. When the chorus came, I sang the words softly to her, "And he walks with me, and he talks with me, and he tells me I am his own. And the joy we share as we tarry there, none other has ever known."

Lynn played the closing notes to the song just as I finished the woman's nails. I placed her hands in her lap, and she stared down at them. "Thank you for letting me paint them," I said. She stared back at me with a blank expression, and a minute later she shuffled her wheelchair away to another section of the dining room.

"Thank you for doing that," Philip said. "She doesn't understand much anymore, and I've never seen her sit so still—usually she's grabbing at my arm." I told Philip it must be because he's such a good friend. Philip gave a small nod and a smile that seemed a bit sad.

Just then, a spunky, slender woman with yellow hair and drawn-on eyebrows tapped me on the shoulder. "Are you here to do nails?" she asked/demanded to know.

"Yes!" I said. "Would you like me to paint yours?"

"Well, look at them!" was her emphatic reply as she held up her hands in front of me. Her nails were purple and slightly chipped. I let her pick her own color and then got down to work. As I clipped and filed, she chatted constantly and watched every move I made.

Philip piped up from his side of the table. "My wife died

last Christmas. We were married sixty-seven years." I could hear both the sadness and the love in his simple statement.

"What was her name?" I asked.

"Carolina." He said it with such tenderness that I had to swallow back tears.

As soon as Philip finished talking, my spunky client started chatting again. She was divorced, she wanted me to know, and had three children. One lived in another state, another was sick with a lung disease, and she really hoped the third would come visit her later. I listened and nodded and responded when it was appropriate, but I looked back to Philip from time to time too. He watched Lynn play and finished coloring the LOVE page that the first woman had started. I wished I could rewind time and bring Carolina back for him.

I finished painting spunky woman's nails, and she thanked me. I started to ask her what her name was, but she cut me off and informed me that bingo was about to start. I laughed as she rushed off to secure her seat and her game card.

I began packing up my supplies and watched as Lynn leaned down to hug Philip. "I love you for coming to play for us," he said. She kissed his cheek, told him she loved him too, and then he shuffled his chair over to the bingo table. He greeted people as they entered the room, offering friendship and kindness and care to all. He was so generous and so loving . . . and so lonely.

My heart ached that there wasn't anything I could do to alleviate his pain. But pain such as Philip's loss isn't a cavity in need of filling . . . it's a broken heart in need of time.

Most of us aren't very good about giving our time to hurting people. Instead, we try to think of all the things we can say and do to make it better. When our words and actions don't make things better, we eventually give up, wander off, and say and do nothing. Weeks pass and the height of the crisis fades for us. We stop calling or texting or bringing meals. We move on and wish everyone else would too. But it isn't our job to fix broken hearts—it's our job to see them, validate them, and sit with them for however long it takes to heal. Even if it takes a lifetime.

Have we forgotten Jesus in the Garden of Gethsemane, seeking strength for the task at hand, full of dread for what was coming? Have we forgotten that all he asked of his friends was to stay awake with him and pray? Have we forgotten that every time he went to check, they were asleep? Have we forgotten the Jesus who said, "Could you not stay awake with me one hour?" (Matthew 26:40 NRSV). When I look at this passage, I feel a mix of comfort and conviction. I'm comforted in knowing that Jesus was lonely too. And I'm convicted as I wonder, *Whom have I failed to sit with for even one hour?*

Several years ago, I came across a documentary as I was scrolling through Netflix. Narrated by Nicole Kidman, *God Grew Tired of Us* is the story of the "Lost Boys" from Sudan. During the Second Sudanese Civil War (1983–2005), an estimated twenty thousand boys, some as young as three, fled their war-torn country on foot.[1] The boys featured in the film had traveled together for five years, forming makeshift families along the way to protect and support one another from the elements, wild animals, starvation, and soldiers. Less than half survived, but the ones who did landed in a UN refugee camp in Kakuma, Kenya. Their affection for one another was clear, as was their desire for more out of life.

The documentary is less about life in the refugee camp and more about the journeys of three young men who were resettled in America. They were among the 3,800 Lost Boys who were selected in 2001 to start a new life in the United States. The three were named John, Daniel, and Panther. All three had challenges to work through, but John and Panther adjusted fairly well and set up lives most Americans would deem "successful." Today, John is married, has three children, and has won numerous awards for his humanitarian efforts. Panther is also married, and while it took three years to bring his wife to the States, they now live in Pennsylvania with their two children. Panther holds advanced degrees in accounting and leadership and works at a bank. But it's Daniel's story that has stuck with me.

In footage captured at the refugee camp in Kenya, Daniel stands out because he is joyful, full of personality, and possesses a great sense of humor. At the beginning of the film, I was most excited to see what life in America would look like for Daniel. But of the three young men, it ends up being Daniel who struggles most to adjust to life in the United States.

In one particularly poignant scene, Daniel is sitting on a bus stop bench and explaining to someone behind the camera how odd it is that people don't seem to care for each other in America. He saw a woman crying at the bus stop and wondered why no one stopped to ask her if she was okay. In another scene, a separate group of the Lost Boys are walking together to a convenience store to get snacks—traveling in a group just as they did through Sudan and Ethiopia and into Kenya. But their group makes people nervous, and the police tell them not to go to the store in groups anymore. Daniel wonders at the fact that neighbors in America don't know each other. He's lonely and he says so . . . many times.

We don't do well with the lonely stories. We prefer the success stories. We like hearing about the refugees who work three jobs while completing college courses and manage to build a middle-class life in spite of all their hardships. It's harder to hear from someone like Daniel, who experiences life in our culture as isolating and lonely. "You're born for others, and others are born for you," Daniel says, trying to make sense of a culture that makes no sense to him—and implying that maybe American culture doesn't offer as much as we might think it does.[2]

As small children, Daniel and the other Lost Boys fled their homes and walked for thousands of miles, sometimes surviving on leaves and muddy water from puddles or their own urine. They were ambushed by rebel soldiers and attacked by wild animals. They made it to one refugee camp in Ethiopia, only to flee again when war broke out in that country. By the time Daniel came to America, he had spent nearly his entire childhood and adolescent life fleeing or living in a refugee camp. Even so, when we meet him in Kakuma, there is a light in his eyes and a bright smile that covers his face. But by the time the camera pans to him in America, that light has dimmed and there's a sadness in Daniel's eyes. He and his companions had survived war, disease, famine, and lions because they banded together in community—that was the key that kept them alive. And now it was gone. How would he survive the loneliness? Or maybe the bigger question is, how do we?

In our middle-class Western world, we don't have to fight to survive, and that is a gift. And yet, it's hard not to wonder if we've lost something too. Maybe, as Mother Teresa said, "We have forgotten that we belong to each other."

It was a warm summer evening when I heard a loud bang followed by total silence. John would soon be home from work, and I had been gathering ingredients in the kitchen, preparing to cook our family a simple dinner. My kids were in the living room watching whatever their movie of the month was. It was an ordinary evening, closing out what had been a series of quite ordinary days.

When the TV suddenly went black, Mareto and Arsema jumped up with startled expressions on their faces. It was strangely quiet—the usual hum of all our electrical appliances was gone. The power was out. Given the loud bang, I didn't have a lot of hope that the electricity would flicker back on any time soon, so the kids and I put on our shoes and wandered down the street to find our friends in their front yard with their own young children.

The kids played while we parents talked about nothing in particular. Soon, more and more people emerged from their homes and wandered down the street asking the same question, "Do you have power?" Someone finally called the electric company and informed us that the loud bang had been the sound of a large transformer blowing—the entire neighborhood was without power.

I was thankful it was summer—still light out and warm. Oh well, we agreed, we'll just sit outside since no electricity meant no working air conditioners or fans. The kids were having a blast together anyway, so we'd just enjoy this small break from the normal evening routine. It wasn't long before John's car came around the curve at the top of the hill and stopped in front of us. I walked to the driver's-side window and explained what had happened. He parked in front of our home, went inside to change out of his uniform, and a few minutes later came walking down the street to join us— barefoot and wearing shorts and a T-shirt.

Soon another friend from up the street came into view, pushing a stroller in front of her. She waved and called out a warm hello in her thick Ghanaian accent. My children squealed in delight at the sight of her and rushed to coo over her daughter, whom they adore. Arsema is so smitten and devoted, she is now referred to as "big sister." I delight in being called "Auntie." There were more greetings and hugs and explanations of what happened to the electricity. Bob, an elderly man who lives alone, came out of his house hold- ing a fistful of Tootsie Pops for the kids. He smiled as they each politely thanked him before tearing off the wrappers and shoving the trash into parents' pockets and the suckers into their mouths. And that's pretty much how the evening went. We laughed and chatted and watched the children play.

After a couple of hours, the sun was getting low and the kids were getting hungry. We slowly wandered back up the street to our own home and fed the kids peanut butter and jelly sandwiches for dinner. Later, after an involuntary treasure hunt for batteries to power their white-noise machines, the kids were tucked into bed, and John and I ate takeout by candlelight. We talked about how fun it had been to gather outside with our friends for a lazy evening and even meet new people we didn't realize lived nearby. I joked that it might be nice if the power went out about once a week so we could gather together more often. John's face got serious as he agreed.

Later, as I was lying in bed listening to the sound of our own white-noise machine, I thought about the turn of events that evening and my conversation with John over dinner. We had all truly enjoyed leaving the routine of our homes for a couple of hours and simply gathering together to connect. Why didn't we do this more often? Why did it take a transformer blowing to coax us out of our homes and into each other's front yards and lives?

In all our day-to-day busyness, distractions, and even complacency, we are missing out on something vital: each other. We don't know who lives in our neighborhoods because we're too absorbed with what's happening within our own walls or on our screens to venture out. As I considered this, I felt a bit like an ostrich with her head stuck in the sand who suddenly looks up and discovers what she's been missing. What did I actually know about my neighbors and what is happening in their lives? Whose heart is breaking a block away? Whose family just fell apart? Who just took in a foster child? Who had to admit their parent into a nursing home? Who just went to the hospital?

In interviews after the release of *God Grew Tired of Us*, Daniel stressed our need for others. "Without them, the world is lonely," he said. "When something happens to you, don't leave it for yourself, give it to others."[3]

Do we recognize the lonely among us when we rush by them? Do we recognize the loneliness in ourselves, or have we masked it with routines, activities, and to-do lists? If we slow down and intentionally step into each other's lives, we will cultivate empathy for our neighbors that can combat the loneliness epidemic in our communities. How can we see people, understand them, and feel with them if we're constantly running past them or jumping to the next event? Empathy, like love, is patient. It takes time.

When we call out "Hi! How are you?" as we pass each other on the street, in the store, or in the church hallways, we can pause and turn it from a mindless greeting into a sincere question as we wait for the answer and linger long enough to ask follow-up questions.

When we see someone looking sad, confused, or downcast on the bus bench or in the office breakroom, we can stop to ask, "Are you okay?" and then stick around to listen and offer assistance or simply friendship.

When we're in the middle of a recipe and realize we're short two eggs, instead of grabbing the keys and running to the store, we might consider knocking on our neighbor's door and asking if they have a couple of eggs to spare, then returning later with a plate of warm cookies to enjoy together.

If we've lost our sense of togetherness, it's because we have learned to rush from one thing to the next, mind our own business, and live a life "looking out for number one." In doing so, we become a society of number ones . . . the loneliest number that you'll ever be, as the song goes. A life that focuses on nothing but our own interests is a life void of empathy. But a life rich in community, focused on others, is a life that is naturally and continually building empathy in ourselves and those around us . . . which becomes a life overflowing in neighbor love.

May we not wait for the transformer to blow before we step into each other's lives and just sit with one another—whether it's in the nursing home, the front yard, or at the bus stop.

# TUNING OUR HEARTS TO THE STORIES AROUND US

A riot is the language of the unheard.
MARTIN LUTHER KING JR.

A couple of years ago, for five excruciating minutes, Mareto went missing during a Sunday afternoon church picnic. It was the end of August and unbearably hot and humid. Mareto had complained of the heat and asked to go home several times—the sun was too bright and there were too many people. Each time he leaned against me and repeated his request, I managed to distract him with some activity. The final distraction was a game of Frisbee with a group of college students.

I was talking with a friend and watching Mareto toss the round disc and then run after it when our daughter ran up to tell me, "Go potty!" I quickly called to John, who was deeply engaged in conversation, and with his nod, Arsema and I hurried off toward the restrooms. When we came out, I casually walked back to the friend I'd been talking with and simultaneously scanned the field for Mareto. When my quick scan failed to locate him, I stepped away from the conversation to look around more thoroughly. Nothing.

Still fairly calm, I called back to John, "Where's Mareto?"

"He said he needed to go to the bathroom, too, and followed you guys," came the response. I shook my head to let John know that Mareto hadn't come into the bathroom with us, and John immediately ran to the men's restroom to check on our son. I relaxed. But then John came back through the door by himself. Mareto wasn't in the bathroom. A bolt of adrenaline shot through my veins.

The picnic location wasn't huge, but it was surrounded by a thick section of overgrown trees, and just behind those trees was a river that is quite deep in some places. We were surrounded by water, and my son couldn't swim. My heart and my mind raced while I tried to clear my head and think about what to do next.

*Water first*, I thought. I ran to the edge of the field where I could see into the trees and quickly walked along the perimeter calling Mareto's name. Soon other people noticed, and I heard someone stop the Frisbee game and say, "Hey, guys, we need to help her find her little boy." I turned and saw nearly everyone in attendance fanning out, some people running, most heading for the water or tree line. It felt like I was in one of those slow-motion movie scenes where the camera zooms in on a person's face and circles around her before panning back out. I began to panic.

*This isn't happening. This can't be real. Oh my gosh, this is real. Why would he run off? Where did he go? What do I do?*

I ran back toward the bathrooms, thinking perhaps he'd somehow snuck into the women's room without me noticing. I bent down to look under the stalls. Nothing. Meanwhile, John had sprinted off to another area of the park where he'd taken the kids fishing in the past. Perhaps Mareto had decided to go back there on his own.

I came out of the bathroom and stood in the parking lot for a brief moment before deciding I couldn't wait any longer—we were losing precious minutes, and I was losing my mind. It was time to call 911. I broke into a run, back toward my purse to get my phone, and got halfway across the parking lot when a voice called out. "He's in the back of your car!" I whirled around to see a friend calmly walking toward me and repeating, "I found him—he's in the back seat."

I ran to our van and opened the door to find Mareto climbing over the seat toward me. The look on his face showed he thought he might be in trouble. I sunk down, grabbed him into my arms, and broke into huge sobs. Shaking and gasping through my tears, I clung to him tightly. Mareto was confused and worried about my reaction, but he was safe. He had simply gotten overwhelmed with all the people and heat and light and decided to take a break in the van without telling us.

As I knelt on the floor of that van, clinging to my son,

I heard echoes of the same call go out from one voice to another, "We found him!" The calls went out one by one, getting fainter with each announcement. A minute later, John came running to the side of the car, panting. A friend brought Arsema over with a soft, "She was worried about her brother," before quietly slipping away. The four of us huddled together in the van while I cried into Mareto's head of curls. When he leaned back with a puzzled expression to look at my face, all I could utter was a shaken, "I thought you were lost."

For the next several hours, I felt sick to my stomach and my hands shook from the rise and release of adrenaline. That night I kept turning those five horrifying minutes over and over in my mind. When I thought back to Mareto's exhausted requests to get out of the bright heat and away from all the people, it made sense that he would seek refuge in the van. While not any cooler, it was out of the sun and away from the people. He'd asked to go home over and over again, and the van is how we get back home. Why hadn't I looked there first?

It struck me that I hadn't really been listening when he told me what was bothering him and what he needed. Instead, I brushed off his concerns and distracted him with activities. He could have stayed in the back of that hot van for another twenty minutes and gotten heat stroke. I shuddered at the thought. I closed my eyes and sighed out a prayer of gratitude that the day had ended with Mareto safe and sleeping in his bed. *Listen better next time,* I thought.

I got my chance a few months later. We were at the playground after school, which is our routine every day that the weather permits. Standing a few yards back, I chatted with the other moms while the kids ran, jumped, tagged, spun, and climbed. In the jumble of jackets and sneakers, I lost sight of Mareto. When I scanned the playground and still couldn't find him, I called Arsema over. "Where's your brother?" I asked. She shrugged and ran off to continue playing. I stood for a moment and thought. It was cold and he was tired from a long day at school. I hurried toward our van and, sure enough, there was Mareto, settling into his car seat and reaching for the seat belt. He looked back at me and simply stated, "I'm cold. I want to go home." I knew where to look for him because I'd been listening and learning to see the world as Mareto did. I'd come to understand what his needs were and that there was purpose behind his actions.

How many times, though, have I failed to be there for the people in my neighborhood because I haven't been listening to them or I've rushed in with my own voice too soon? Listening cultivates empathy for others because it gives us glimpses of their world—their experiences, their pain and joy and hopes and fears. It's how we step out of our own shoes and learn what life is like in the shoes of another. The challenge is that we live in a culture of quick fixes and easy remedies, which means that slow and attentive listening often takes a back seat to immediate action. Because we under-value listening—and thus underutilize it—we lose a vital skill that enables us to love our neighbors well. Worse still, when we haven't allowed listening and empathy to do its long-form work in our hearts and minds, rushing to action can pour salt instead of balm in open wounds.

In her book *I'm Still Here*, Austin Channing Brown gives a powerful illustration of what happens when we jump to speak or act without taking the time to truly listen. In celebration of MLK Day, she and a friend were at a predominantly white church giving a presentation in which she shared sobering experiences of racism, and both women described the origins of their racial reconciliation work together. When the service ended, several white people lined up to confess their own words and acts of racism. One after the other, they laid their burdens on her shoulders. One man had used the N-word, a woman had looked the other way when a coworker was mistreated, and on it went. With each confession, the weight of their burdens increased on Brown.

"None of these confessions involved me," she writes. "But after I had heard all of those confessions, it felt personal. It felt like I was sitting at the table when the racist joke was made. . . . It felt that way because for every confessor, my body had become the stand-in for the actual people who had been harmed in those situations. I was left with the weight of these moments I hadn't experienced."[1] The intentions behind the confessions may have been sincere, but the impact was harmful.

What might have happened if the people who had been gifted with Brown's story had chosen to continue listening and learning rather than rush to unload their confessions? What if they had prioritized learning more from Brown over seeking relief for their guilt? Perhaps seeking to understand would have eventually led to an understanding of the damage such proxy confessions can do. Perhaps Brown would have been spared the burden of their words and those who had actually been wronged by the confessors might have been gifted with the healing words of a heartfelt confession and apology. The confessors may have been sincere in their desire to love their neighbor, but their words and actions were harmful because they failed to listen first and act later. Listening first is an ongoing lesson I am doing my best to learn and practice.

I'm a member of a large Facebook group dedicated to racial reconciliation called Be the Bridge.[2] There is a strict policy of silence for at least three months for all new members. This period isn't meant to be spent quietly waiting, biding our time until we can finally jump in with our opinions and comments. No, we're asked to spend those months doing two things: working through a fairly rigorous curriculum and listening to the others in the group. There are articles to read, videos to watch, podcasts to listen to, and all the while a running thread of topics being discussed with insight and nuance. I've been a member of this group for far longer than three months and have yet to utter a word. I am keenly aware that three months isn't enough time for me—I have much more listening and learning to do.

There is such wisdom in inviting people to listen before joining in a discussion as sensitive and important as racial justice. I don't know if these parameters were put in place at the founding of the group or after some unfortunate discussions that would have been prevented by some preemptive listening. Either way, preemptive listening is what I'm learning daily.

What if we made preemptive listening a lifestyle, the very foundation for loving others? What if we could live out the wisdom written by James: "My dear brothers and sisters, take note of this: Everyone should be quick to listen, slow to speak and slow to become angry" (James 1:19 NIV)? Sadly, and to the detriment of our neighbors, we have inverted this guidance. Instead, we are slow to listen, quick to speak, and even quicker to become angry.

Recently I was talking with an acquaintance about current events—tricky waters to navigate in today's polarized climate—but so far, we'd been able to discuss things openly and respectfully, so I wasn't too worried. I was startled when the conversation took a sharp turn from the topic we'd been discussing to something new, because we'd not been even remotely near the zip code of the new topic. Trying to keep up with the change in direction, I listened intently until there was a long pause and it was clear she was looking for my response. Carefully and calmly, I said, "Well, I don't agree with that . . ." I got less than two words into my explanation before I was cut off and treated to what can only be described as a tirade. Arms flew up and down, fingers pointed, the volume significantly increased, and I wondered how she had any air left, because I hadn't heard her take a breath. The conversation ended abruptly when she decided she had said her piece and it was over. As I watched her walk away, I felt stunned and a little bulldozed.

It took me several hours to shake off the interaction. I tried to identify what I could have done differently that might have prevented her outburst, but all that flashed before me was her waving arms and a fuming voice. The more I thought about it, the more I realized that what upset me most was feeling I had been silenced. I hadn't been given the respect of being heard, and it hurt because the topic she'd raised was deeply personal to me. I hadn't expected to change her mind, but I did hope to share a perspective she might not have considered. I don't know if I'll ever get an opportunity to share my thoughts and experience on this topic with her, but if not, our relationship will always be stunted.

Are we willing to hear what our neighbors are trying to tell us, even when it makes us uncomfortable? Or are we determined to remain in the comfort of our echo chambers—letting our own voices reverberate off the walls of our living rooms, social media accounts, and communities? That's a choice we get to make every day. We can choose to listen and learn and ask rather than point and accuse. We can choose to slow down, dig deeper, and attend to another's heart. We can choose to see things from a perspective other than our own.

Last summer, my book club read *Born a Crime* by comedian Trevor Noah. I was fascinated by his stories of growing up a mixed-race child in South Africa during apartheid. I also learned a lot. One of the chapters I underlined most was titled, "Go Hitler!" In it, Noah describes a period of time after high school in which he worked as a disc jockey at local parties and events. Part of what made this venture such a success was a member of Noah's crew whose job was to get everyone at the party up and dancing. This dancer's unfortunate name was Hitler.

One day, Noah and his crew were invited to DJ during a culture day event being held at a Jewish school. They set up and got the party started—he played hip-hop hits and Hitler got the crowds dancing. As he danced, the other members of Noah's group gathered around Hitler in a circle, as they had at numerous other events, and began chanting his name, "Go, Hitler! Go, Hitler! Go, Hitler!" The room stopped. Jewish children, teachers, and parents all froze, horrified. But Noah and his group didn't know what the problem was. Why was everyone upset?

A yelling match with a teacher ensued. She called Noah and his friends disgusting and vile and used the term "you people," which is such a loaded phrase that Noah immediately assumed the attack to be racist. Noah responded by yelling back that they were free now and wouldn't be stopped. Still screaming, Noah packed up the gear, and he and his crew marched away from the event chanting, "Go, Hitler! Go, Hitler! Go, Hitler!"

I read this entire exchange, cringing at the awful misunderstanding of it all. Noah and the rest of his group didn't know that the name Hitler was offensive (to say the absolute least) to Jewish people. Apartheid had attempted to strip black people of their education, and they hadn't gone to schools heavily influenced by Western culture and history. They didn't mean to hurt; they simply didn't know. Noah wrote that his own grandfather thought Hitler was the name of a type of army tank that was helping Germany win the war.

The section I highlighted most in that chapter was not the story itself or what Noah didn't know at the time, but what *I* didn't know. Here is how Noah describes the misunderstanding:

There is also this to consider: The name Hitler does not offend a black South African because Hitler is not the worst thing a black South African can imagine. Every country thinks their history is the most important, and that's especially true in the West. But if black South Africans could go back in time and kill one person, Cecil Rhodes would come up before Hitler. If people in the Congo could go back in time and kill one person, Belgium's King Leopold would come way before Hitler. If Native Americans could go back in time and kill one person, it would probably be Christopher Columbus or Andrew Jackson.[3]

I had to google Cecil Rhodes and King Leopold, because I didn't know who they were or why their names might draw a collective shudder from entire nations of people. I was an adult before I learned the atrocities Christopher Columbus had committed against the Indigenous Peoples of the Americas, which eventually led to genocide. One truth pounds me again and again like a hammer: *I will never reach a day when I can stop listening, stop reading, stop watching, and stop learning.* To have any hope of loving my neighbors well, I have to recognize that the depths of human suffering stretch well beyond my geography, my culture, and my life span.

I have been blogging now for over a decade, sharing bits of my life with anyone who cares to visit my website. Recently I went through all my old blog posts with a critical eye to take down anything I don't want living on the internet. It was an eye-opening project, and I hardly recognized myself in some of the words I'd written ten years ago. As I worked through each post, putting some in the trash bin, making others private, and leaving some public, I saw how much I've changed and grown over the years. I wondered at the shifts in my perspective and realized that, somewhere along the way, I started listening.

I removed certain posts because I started listening to adult adoptees and no longer wanted certain pictures or details of my children and their adoption experience available for public consumption. I took down posts that centered my experience as a parent of disabled children because I started listening to disabled adults. I deleted devotional posts that were void of any nuance and had failed to consider marginalized people because I'd since learned how they had been hurt by the distortion of certain scriptures. It was a refining process and one I'm sure I will repeat over the years as I continue to tune my ears to the wisdom and perspectives of others.

❧

I began playing the violin when I was ten years old. I am certain that my first year or so was a lesson in patience for my parents as they endured me screeching my way through such hits as "Hot Cross Buns" and "Mary Had a Little Lamb."

As time passed and I honed my skills, my practice times sounded less like a goat slowly dying and more like music. To train my ear and teach me how to tune my own violin strings, a teacher gave me a silver tuning fork. I tapped it against my desk or a book and held it up to my violin to hear the hum of a perfect A note. Tilting my head toward the tuning fork, I alternated between running the bow along my A string and twisting the pegs at the scroll of my instrument. There I'd sit, ears perked to the sound of the tuning fork, hands working to match its pitch. Over time, this little exercise trained my ear to the point that I no longer needed the tuning fork. I knew what an A should sound like, and I tuned my violin to the sound that had carved deep grooves into the music corner of my mind.

Learning to love our neighbors is a little like learning to tune a violin. We have to listen before we can love. We must tilt our heads and tune our ears to the stories they share and the needs they express. It requires patience and practice. Learning from and listening to our neighbors cultivates empathy within us, which enables us to love well. So many hurt feelings, shouting matches, unnecessary offenses, and harmful actions could be avoided if we all tuned our ears to one another.

# SIX

# THE MAGIC OF *WHAT IF?*

True change takes place in the imagination.
THOMAS MOORE

I was ten years old and living in Poway, California, when a domestic terrorist parked a truck full of explosives in front of the Alfred P. Murrah Federal Building in downtown Oklahoma City and blew it up. The next morning, I walked to school, entered my classroom, took off my backpack, and settled in at my desk. My classmates were talking back and forth in a quick string of stories, and the hushed but energetic conversations soon caught my attention. Everyone knew about the bombing—everyone except me.

"Hundreds of people got killed."

"I heard it was more. Maybe a thousand!"

"A bunch of kids died too. I saw it on TV."

"I saw a lot of smoke and black stuff all over people. Lots of blood too."

With these snippets of information from my ten-year-old peers, I pieced together that a bomb had exploded somewhere and a lot of people had died. I still remember the cold, clammy feeling in my hands. Soon my teacher realized that no one would be able to focus on lessons, so she called the class to attention and allowed us to talk, process, and ask questions.

One by one, kids raised their hands and shared things they'd seen on television and in the newspaper, and snippets they'd overheard from parents at the kitchen table or on the radio on the way to school. With every bit of information, a picture formed in my head: bleeding children, shards of glass, twisted steel, broken buildings, and broken bodies. Fear and confusion and panic coursed through me.

Eventually, I got up from my desk and walked up to my teacher, who was sitting at the front of the classroom. "I'm scared," I said. "I don't want to talk about this anymore—I'm going to have nightmares." She was gentle in her response, asking me to step outside the classroom. She joined me a few moments later, and then my memory blurs. Someone—the office secretary, the nurse, or my teacher— called my mom. The next thing I remember is sitting in the front passenger seat of our car while my mom explained what had happened in Oklahoma City the day before.

I was upset. I couldn't shake the images my classmates' descriptions had conjured in my mind. My imagination projected a steady stream of horror before me, and I didn't sleep well for several nights. Around this time my parents bought a new minivan and, to this day, whenever I get a whiff of new-car smell, my mind zooms me back to 1995 and newsreel images of the Oklahoma City bombing.

I have a very active imagination. Say a word, and my mind cooks up an image as vivid as if it were real life. And it isn't a vague thought that skips by; it's as detailed as a 3D movie, and it doesn't go away. I can clearly visualize all kinds of events and scenarios. This strange superpower has contributed heavily to my anxiety over the years. In any given situation, I can ask myself, *What if?* and then imagine every possible answer to that question. For example . . .

We're at the park, and I watch my children play—flinging their bodies around equipment, running with ease, tripping, and then bouncing back up as they laugh and take off running once more. My daughter begins to climb a jungle gym, and I'm suddenly afraid. *What if she falls?* I can picture the broken bones and the scream-filled drive to the emergency room. My muscles tense, my heart rate quickens, and before I can catch myself, my arms begin to reach out to catch her nonexistent fall.

We're driving over a bridge, and I ask myself, *What if the bridge collapses or there's an accident?* Then I rehearse each and every step I might take to get us out of danger.

We're in a crowded public space, and I cling too tightly to my children's hands as I wonder, *What if I lose track of them?*

If I'm not careful, my anxiety can allow the what-ifs to rule my life.

When I returned to my classroom the day after my mom had picked me up from school, a few of my peers asked, "Are you scared? Is that why you left?" I was self-conscious

and insisted I was fine—just not feeling well. "I had to go to
the nurse, that's all." I felt ashamed of my fear, my sadness,
and the heavy feeling of being overwhelmed by terror in
the world. It's the first time I remember being embarrassed
about my extra-sensitive nature.

Many times I've wished I could grow calluses on my
heart and mind so the harder parts of life wouldn't hurt so
much. I've wondered how others seem to navigate life without feeling crushed by all the heartbreak in the world. How
did everyone else wake up and go to school and work on
September 12, 2001, the day after terrorists crashed planes
into the World Trade Center and the Pentagon? How did the
world keep turning after the Oklahoma City bombing, or
Hurricane Katrina, or the 2010 earthquake in Haiti? I felt
emotionally overwhelmed by all of these events. At times
I've tried telling myself, *Toughen up!* I've tried to convince
myself that it serves no purpose to absorb the pain around
me like a sponge. But then I learned something that gave me
a whole new perspective.

I first heard of ideational behavior in a counselor's office.
It was one of several times we were discussing something
that made me anxious. My counselor explained that some
people have a very strong and active imagination. We can
hear something, immediately conjure up a mental image,
and—this is the key—hold it there. It can be a wonderful
tool, a gift, he told me. I understood what he meant, but it
doesn't ever feel that way.

When I read a headline about a child dying in a border detention center, it doesn't feel like a gift when I immediately picture my own eight-year-old son in his place. I see him sick and shivering and scared. His eyes are vacant and frightened and despairing all at once. My heart lurches, and I want to crawl out of my skin, because I am nearly losing my mind at the thought of my son hurting and alone without me there to hold, comfort, and reassure him.

When I hear about another school shooting on the radio, it doesn't feel like a gift when I imagine my terrified daughter huddled under her first-grade desk and the fear coursing through her veins while I am miles away and helpless to stop it.

When I read another article about an unarmed black teenager who was shot and killed by the police, it doesn't feel like a gift when I glance over at my tall-for-his-age black son playing in the pool with a small water gun, and my mind melds the two stories together. Suddenly it's him with the toy, not Tamir Rice, and my gut lurches to my chest as I try to shake the image of my own child lying facedown for no reason at all except that white supremacy still kills.

All the bad news, the death and destruction and tragedy of the world, plays like a movie in my mind, and the people I love have the starring roles. I don't really see the positives here; it just hurts.

But I listen as my counselor tells me that people who exhibit ideational behavior make wonderful artists and musicians and creatives. He acknowledges the negative side, the anxiety and panic that can take over if left unchecked, but then he says the word that sticks. People with this personality type have a strong ability to offer *empathy*. Now I am intrigued. Perhaps what I have considered a curse might truly be a gift with purpose. If my what-ifs could make me run *from* the world, could the opposite also be true? Could my what-ifs help me run *toward* the world instead?

- What if it were my child who was sick, cold, and alone? What would love look like to me then?
- What if I were struggling to pay the mortgage and buy groceries? What would love do for me then?
- What if I were caught in the cycle of addiction? How might love set me free?
- What if I lost my husband to violence? How would love grieve with me?
- What if I were being persecuted by authority figures? How would love fight for justice?
- What if everywhere I looked, doors were being slammed in my face? How would love open them?

Imagination is a tool, and just like any other tool, it can be used to destroy or create. If we let imagination feed our anxiety, it will cripple us. But if we cultivate our imagination as a way to feed and grow our empathy, we can build relationships and forge new paths to our neighbors. We can love.

It turns out that science agrees. Recent research supports the idea that an active imagination can compel us to reach out to our neighbors. One study found that "the more vivid an imagined event was, the greater the willingness to interact."[1] In other words, imagination has the power to cultivate empathy when we can picture ourselves inside someone else's story or situation. Maybe this is part of the reason Jesus so often taught in parables. He wanted his listeners to see the world in a new way—through the eyes of another.

If the greatest commandment Christ gives us is to love God and love our neighbors, it makes sense that his teaching style would use stories rather than abstract principles. When crowds grumbled about Jesus eating with tax collectors and others they considered undesirables, Jesus didn't look them in the eye and say, "Here's the principle: every human being is valuable and matters to God." He told them a story about one lost sheep and a shepherd who left the ninety-nine to find the one. He told them about a woman losing a coin in her home and turning the whole place upside down to get it back. He painted a word picture of a son who betrays his father, squanders his inheritance, and hits rock bottom, but is still welcomed home by a father who runs out to embrace him. What parent can't picture themselves in that story? As a mom, I know that there is nothing my children could do to make me not love them.

When Jesus saw the self-righteousness of religious authorities who heaped judgment and scorn on others, he told the story of a humble tax collector. When his own disciples wanted to put a limit on forgiveness, he told them the story of a servant who owed his master an enormous sum of money. When the servant couldn't pay, the master ordered him sold along with his wife and children. But the servant fell to his knees, begging forgiveness and grace. The master had compassion on him and forgave the debt.

The servant then went to his fellow servant who owed him a small amount of money and tried to beat it out of him, refused him mercy, and had him thrown in jail. The imagery is enough. We get that one is wrong and the other right. We feel disgust and anger at the hypocrisy of the unforgiving servant—and this is the point. Our empathy peaks, and we instinctively understand how to love our neighbors better.

And when a lawyer looks for a loophole by asking, "Who is my neighbor?", Jesus tells the story of a man beaten and left for dead, and how two men pass him by but a third does not. The Samaritan gives of his time, his money, his donkey, his clothing, his shelter, and his friendship. The story stirs something in our hearts, and we know deep down, even before we read the next words in the story, what the answer is to the lawyer's question. We know who our neighbor is. Imagination has guided us through to empathy.

❦

Recently my children studied Christopher Columbus in school. I was interested to know how this now-controversial historical figure would be portrayed.

"Who was Christopher Columbus?" I asked my son.

"He was really good at sailing," Mareto said. But then he gave the answer I had been dreading: "He discovered America."

I paused, found my mental footing, and tried to add more context to the story. "Did you know that there were already thriving civilizations here before Columbus arrived in the Americas?"

My own elementary school education was woefully inadequate in this area. I'd learned about the Spanish conquests in Central and North America in particular. The version of history I was taught was far rosier than reality. We learned little phrases and rhymes to help us remember the Niña, the Pinta, and the Santa Maria. My elementary school peers and I sang, "In the year of 1492, Columbus sailed the ocean blue," to burn the date in our brains for all of eternity. It wasn't until my freshman year of college, when I took a class from an indigenous professor of history, that I heard a very different view of our nation's founding story.

That's when I learned about the genocide of Indigenous Peoples and the horrors their children experienced when forced to attend Catholic boarding schools. When I did additional research on my own, I learned that Christopher Columbus was responsible for the enslavement, torture, and murder of untold numbers of Indigenous Peoples. And only when I started reading and listening to Indigenous men and women themselves did I begin to understand the persecution, erasure, and struggles they face to this day.

I can still remember the catchy tune that reminds me of the year Columbus arrived in the Americas, but now it makes me queasy because I know the jagged scars that 1492 arrival left in its wake. Fifty-six million Indigenous People would die over the next one hundred years. A holocaust just as merciless, just as horrifying, as Hitler's Nazi regime.[2]

It wasn't until recent years that I understood how shameful it is that we have sports teams with names that are racial slurs and mascots that are harmful caricatures of Indigenous Peoples. In fact, in my younger years, I didn't consider them racist at all. And all the while we continue to celebrate Columbus Day as a federal holiday.

I wanted my children to understand the truth about Christopher Columbus early. Right away. So I asked both the kids another question, "Was Christopher Columbus a good man or a bad man?"

Mareto answered without hesitation, "Bad." Arsema nodded in agreement. I was pleasantly surprised.

"Why is that?" I asked.

Mareto's response was eight-year-old simple. "Because he was mean to Native Americans."

I nodded my agreement as I looked at my children's furrowed brows. They were reciting things they'd heard at school, but they didn't really understand. I tried to explain further about stolen land, disease, and murder. But their confusion grew until my husband chimed in with a parable, and he started with the magic word: *imagine.*

Imagine you and your friends are learning, playing, laughing, and sharing meals together at school. You're a family, right? This is your school. You all have your schedules and systems, and you are happy there.

Then one day, someone—let's call him Chris—and his own group of friends shows up and says, "Aha! I've discovered a brand-new place for us!" But he hasn't discovered anything new, has he? It's your school and always has been. So, being curious and friendly, you open the door. But instead of joining you in your classrooms and cafeteria and on the playground, Chris and his friends take over the building. They kill your teachers and kick you out. They destroy all your art-work and lessons and projects. They steal some of your friends and make them servants. And the whole time, they claim they're better than you and their way of doing things is better than the way you had been doing things.

You want your school back, don't you? Some of your friends try to get back in the doors, but they're locked. So they grab a hammer and a crowbar and try to take down the doors and break the windows. But Chris and his friends have bigger hammers and better weapons, so they kill your friends. They tell you the only way you can stay at the school is if you speak their language, change your religion to theirs, and do things their way. Otherwise, you're out.

What if that happened at your school? Would it hurt your feelings to have a holiday celebrating Chris each year? Would you want your children and grand-children and their grandchildren to celebrate Chris every year?

We could see the wheels turning in their minds and understanding creep across their faces. Putting themselves into the situation, asking themselves, *What if?* and stoking the flames of their imagination gave them understanding. Imagination is a critical tool, because we weren't there when 1492 and its aftermath happened and we don't know what it feels like to be part of a people group whose perspective and experiences are often erased from the history books and public discourse.

When someone tells us they are hurting, when we learn of a tragedy we've never experienced, when a friend knocks on our door but we haven't walked in her shoes and we don't know what to do or how to respond, we must exercise imagination to jump-start our empathy. We need to practice asking ourselves, *What if?*

- What if my husband just lost his job?
- What if my child was the one with the diagnosis?
- What if I was torn from my parents at three years old?
- What if a tornado leveled my town?
- What if I was the one struggling with crippling depression?
- What if my kids' school had an active shooter roaming the halls?
- What if bombs rained down on our home, our state, our nation?
- What if gangs threatened to kill my parents?

*What if? What if? What if?*

We need to let our minds wander deeper into the myriad of possibilities and struggles and emotions and needs and choices that could happen in the land of what-if. And then, we get to let our imagination lead us into greater empathy for one another, which propels us into the arms and homes and lives of our neighbors, allowing us to love them as we love ourselves.

# BIG FEELINGS LEAD TO BIG LOVE

The greatest gift you ever give is your honest self.
FRED ROGERS

**W**e sped past fields and trees as the school bus, filled with rowdy middle schoolers excited to be heading back home, bounced and jostled with each pothole and groove in the road. I sat straight as a board, eyes forward and avoiding eye contact with anyone, reminding myself that bullies love attention more than anything else. *Ignore her, and she'll stop.*

Behind me was an eighth-grade classmate named Holly who was leaning forward in her seat, singing the Mickey Mouse Club theme song in a mocking voice. Each time she got to the spelling section of the tune, she flicked the back of my head, punctuating each letter. With each flick, I felt my cheeks grow warmer and I blinked back tears, not sure whether I was more horrified by her cruelty or the thought of crying in front of my peers.

I've always had a high-pitched voice. When I was a young newlywed, I couldn't get the concierge to book a hotel room for our weekend away because he didn't believe I was over twenty-one. Telemarketers still ask for my mother when I answer the phone, a high school boyfriend dumped me because the sound of my voice was "too annoying to get past," and in eighth grade, Holly sat behind me on the bus singing the Mickey Mouse Club song while flicking the back of my head.

Eighth grade was a rough year. I was the new girl in school for the third time in three years. I was also smack-dab in the middle of puberty and developing at a rate for which I was not emotionally prepared (and middle school boys aren't exactly known for their tact). To make things just ever so much more excruciating, I was extremely sensitive. I always have been, and I always will be. I cry watching movies and commercials and ten-second home video clips. I avoid watching anything too violent or labeled "thrilling and suspenseful," because I know I'll be up all night replaying the fear-inducing images in my mind. And when someone is cruel, unfair, or unjust, it hurts, and I can't hide it. I wish I'd known in eighth grade what I know now—that sensitivity can be a strength—but I didn't.

When I was a little girl, I loved watching *Mister Rogers' Neighborhood*. It was one of my favorite shows. My mom recently pointed out how interesting it was to see which parts of the show my brother and I enjoyed the most. She said my brother played with toys and barely looked up during the first half of the show, but immediately tuned in when the trolley came to take viewers to the Neighborhood of Make-Believe with Daniel Tiger, King Friday XIII, Lady Elaine, Henrietta, and the others.

I, on the other hand, preferred the first half of the show—the part when we entered into Mister Rogers' home and neighborhood. He welcomed us into his living room with a song and a warm greeting, then he introduced us to his neighbors—the people in his day-to-day world. We'd venture out with him to someplace new and interesting—the crayon factory, a cake contest, a music shop, and so on. I was fascinated by the people we met and the things we learned. It felt like the real world, because in a way it was. These were all the same types of people I met in my day-to-day too. Mister Rogers showed me how valuable and interesting and important our neighbors truly are.

Mister Rogers talked to us about real people and real issues in a simple, loving way. He didn't shy away from conflict or tough and scary issues. Instead, he talked openly about hard things and showed us what it means to be a good neighbor—what it looks like to make the world a better place, one person, one neighborhood, one day at a time.

At a time when kids' television was mainly cartoons and slapstick comedy, Mister Rogers offered a calm, thoughtful, and kind alternative. He encouraged viewers to see the best in themselves and in others. He cooled his feet in a kiddie pool with Officer Clemmons, who was African American, just four months after the assassination of Martin Luther King Jr., and a short five years after a white hotel manager in Florida had poured acid in a pool filled with interracial swimmers. Mister Rogers invited children using wheelchairs to come on his show and talk about their lives in simple and matter-of-fact ways. To this day, watching reruns of *Mister Rogers' Neighborhood* always leaves me feeling that we are all incredibly special, valuable, and unique . . . and yet absolutely ordinary in the best way.

I loved watching the documentary about Fred Rogers' life, *Won't You Be My Neighbor?* I missed seeing it in the theater but watched it in the comfort of my own home when it was released to streaming services. I'm glad for that, because I was crying within the first two minutes of the film. One particular part has stuck with me, and I think about it often.

The film includes interviews with several people who worked with Rogers throughout the years of the show. One segment focuses on some of the ways Mister Rogers was portrayed in pop culture and includes some of his reactions to the various ways people made fun of his show. His colleagues affirmed that he had a good sense of humor, but that sometimes the teasing stung and he didn't find the jokes funny. The screen flashed with images of a young, preteen Fred who was slightly overweight and who was taunted with the name Fat Freddy. His wife, Joanne Rogers, said that he had difficulty making friends as an adolescent and was bullied quite a bit. But it was the response shared by David Newell, who played Mr. McFeely, that has stayed with me.

"I've often wondered, if there hadn't been a 'Fat Freddy,' would there have been a Mister Rogers?"[1]

What if Mister Rogers had denied the hurt and tried to brush off the bullying as no big deal? What if young Fred had swallowed his feelings and accepted the idea of "survival of the fittest" and tried to be tough? Maybe he would have ended up making slapstick comedy instead of thoughtful television episodes in which he sang to children, "It's you I like," and told them that they could be loved just as they are. The thought of a world without the impact of *Mister Rogers' Neighborhood* is awful, and I believe that the only reason that alternate reality doesn't exist is because young Fred embraced his true emotions and, in doing so, was able to extend empathy and love to others in remarkable ways.

The other night I was sitting bedside with one of my children, who had gotten out of bed for the third time since being tucked in. I was tired and frustrated but tried to put that aside as I asked, "Why do you keep getting up?" The response was one I'd heard from this particular child more than once. "I'm just scared, and I don't like being alone and I don't like bedtime. Bedtime is the worst time."

Instead of reassuring my child that such bedtime fears were unfounded, I shared my own experience. I, too, had hated bedtime as a child. Wide eyes stared back at me as I went on to share about my nightmares and fears and struggles with sleep. I kept talking and soon found myself saying, "I know it's hard, but I think that this can be used for good. I think it shows that we have big feelings, and we can use those same big feelings to love other people and make the world better, kinder, and less scary."

Arguably, Fred Rogers made the world better, kinder, and less frightening for many of us. Was a small part of that because he knew the sting of being bullied and taunted and known as Fat Freddy? Is that why he dedicated his life to spreading love and compassion and kindness? Did the big feelings of rejection foster an empathy in young Fred that led to big love? I wonder if I would be the mother I am today if I'd never known restless nights jumping at shadows, the mocking voices singing behind me on the bus, and the stinging humiliation of flicks to the back of my head. Often, the moments of grace and compassion we extend to others find their origins in our most difficult moments.

It was thirteen years ago that my friend's toddler son died suddenly, but I can still picture everything as if it were last year. The phone call came first. It was late in the evening, and we were winding down for bed. John answered as I sat on the edge of our bed, picking at the pink rosettes on the comforter I'd picked out shortly after our wedding. Moments later he hung up and turned to me. "Jonathan has been helicoptered to the UVA hospital with a cerebral hemorrhage."

Even today, thinking back to that moment, I have a similar reaction—my eyes immediately fill with tears, my hands go cold, my heart sinks, and my throat thickens. I remember my response. "That's not good," I whispered. We slept with the phone on the nightstand and waited for news. It came in the morning—Jonathan never regained consciousness and passed away in the arms of his parents. He was two years old. Blond, messy, and full of promise.

Jonathan's mother, Chris, was my close friend. She was nine months pregnant and giving her older children a bath while Jonathan played on the floor next to her. Suddenly, he screamed, grabbed the side of his head, vomited, passed out, and never woke up again. I couldn't process how one moment he'd been a delightful little toddler, marveling at big trucks, and the next he was gone. I was overcome with grief for my friend and didn't know what to do.

After a flurry of phone calls, a group of us put together a plan for the coming days. I would bring food to their home that afternoon and stay to feed and occupy the kids. I busied myself with pot roast, macaroni and cheese, and sides. My nerves were frayed as we pulled into their driveway and parked the car. What would I say? They'd kissed their son goodbye just hours earlier. He'd been perfectly fine less than twenty-four hours ago, and now he was gone. We were all in shock, and I was terrified to walk through the door of their house. I wanted to be supportive and comforting but had no idea what to do, and I desperately wanted to do the right thing—whatever that was.

We walked in, arms full of food, and headed straight for the kitchen. I plugged in the slow cooker and grabbed a cutting board. I'd been in this room countless times and prepared meals together with Chris over and over. I knew where to find the plates and napkins to set out for the kids. Grabbing a knife, I started slicing apples. That's when Chris walked in. Her face was red and swollen, but she smiled at me and thanked me for the meal. I hugged her tightly and whispered how sorry I was. As I did, I could feel the rush of tears, and just before it could escape, I caught the sob in my throat. *Don't you dare cry*, I told myself. *You don't have a right to—he wasn't your son.* Swallowing and blinking hard, I quickly turned back to the cutting board and continued slicing apples. "I'm just putting plates together for the kids," I said, trying to pull myself together. I took a deep breath, shoved my feelings to the side, and asked, "Is there anything I can do to help you right now?"

Chris mentioned she hadn't had a chance to shower and thought it would be nice to get one while the kids ate dinner. I was thrilled. Something tangible for me to do—a simple way to help. "Yes!" I encouraged her. "You go take your time. Get a nice hot shower, and I'll feed and sit with the kids." Off she went, and I went back to the line of plates waiting to be filled.

Over the years, I've thought a lot about my reaction to Jonathan's death and my reaction to seeing Chris in her kitchen that day. Regret is the emotion that usually fills me when I look back. I'd been so worried about doing and saying the right thing that I failed to do the human thing, the empathetic and loving thing. I should have let myself cry. Right there in the kitchen when I wrapped my arms around my friend, I should have released that sob from the depths of my heart and let her do the same with me. I lost an opportunity to show her that Jonathan's death broke us all. That his life and her pain mattered deeply. I should have made space for her to grieve with a friend in that moment if she wanted to. But I didn't.

At the time, I didn't think I had a right to cry. I felt like my job was to be strong and solid and compassionate—to deny my feelings in order to extend sympathy for her pain, rather than to embrace my own emotions in order to offer empathy. It took me awhile to understand that crying with Chris might have been the most loving thing I could have done in that moment.

Nine months later, I was wheeled out of the hospital maternity ward late in the afternoon with a prescription for pain medication and a post-op appointment for the following week. Chris had been my first call that morning—just after 6:00 a.m. I sobbed into the phone, "I think I'm losing the baby, and we don't know what to do." She cried on the phone with me and told me to call the hospital. She brought food that night and made me some tea. My mom came the next day. She walked through the front door, hugged John, and immediately asked, "Where is she?" before turning to see me on the couch. Within three strides she was perched on the side of the cushions with her arms around me as we both cried.

Later in the evening, my dad called to check in and asked to speak to me. I can count on one hand the number of times I've heard or seen my dad cry—or even come remotely close to it. When he asked me how I was doing, I was honest. "My heart is broken," I said. I can close my eyes today and still hear his response. "Yeah . . . a lot of us are heartbroken." His voice caught, and I could hear the thickness of emotion through the phone line.

His sadness, his heartbreak, and his tears meant more to me than any number of the get well and sympathy cards

I received in the following weeks. My mom crying on the couch with me over the loss of a child we'd all wanted so badly meant more to me than all the flowers that filled our home over the next several days. When I called my friend Heather the next day to tell her I'd lost the baby and she immediately burst into tears, that meant more to me than any of the meals delivered in the days I recovered from surgery.

My fear of crying in front of Chris in the wake of Jonathan's passing was well-intentioned but ultimately selfish. While there was a piece of me that worried about centering my own emotions, I was too wrapped up in my reaction. I wanted to do and say the right thing. I failed to consider that I could still center my friend and her pain while joining her in it and crying in the pit of loss with her.

Denying emotions creates distance. When we refuse to embrace our own emotions, we can unintentionally dismiss others in theirs. Our feelings can be an important piece of cultivating empathy and to growing as a human being connected with every other human being. We don't have to be dictated by our emotions, but we can allow them to guide us in our interactions and relationships. We aren't robots, and it does no good to our neighbors when we pretend otherwise.

There's a particularly unfortunate expression of this need to paper over emotions in the Christian community. It takes the form of cold platitudes. When confronted with someone else's suffering, we respond with a chirpy saying or a verse and a pat on the back.

Just lost a child? "God needed another angel in heaven."

Struggling to pay rent and buy groceries? "The LORD

will open for you His good storehouse" (Deuteronomy 28:12 NASB).

Shell-shocked from the revelation of a spouse's infidelity? "God works all things together for good" (Romans 8:28 CEB).

Instead of reciting cold platitudes at suffering people, I wish we'd recite this verse silently and to ourselves: "Jesus wept."

When faced with two sisters mourning the death of their brother, Lazarus, Jesus doesn't tell them Lazarus will rise again, hand them a casserole, and move on to the next town. He joins them in their weeping. He empathizes and shares in their grief with tears of his own (John 11:17–37).

In the weeks, months, and years following my two miscarriages, I grieved deeply and usually alone. The anniversary days of these losses were hard and quiet and lonely. I noted the time that had passed: three years . . . eight years . . . twelve years . . . but the tears sometimes overwhelmed me as if no time at all had passed. I now go weeks, even months, without feeling the pangs of loss like tiny pricks to the soul, but from time to time, I'm still ambushed by the loneliness of grief.

The cold platitudes started within days of my first miscarriage. An older woman came to visit and casually mentioned her own miscarriage. "It was early, first trimester," she said. "I was fine. You'll be fine too." Her offhand comments said in too cheery a tone made me feel small and stupid for being so sad.

Dismissive comments other women made about their own losses were also hard to bear. A couple of years after my miscarriage, a family member mentioned going to the hospital when she started bleeding in her first trimester. "It was just a miscarriage," she said. "I had to pay an emergency room co-pay all for a late period!" She seemed more annoyed by the bill than sad over her loss. Her words hit me like a punch to the gut.

Just recently an acquaintance waved off my words of sorrow for her miscarriage with a breezy, "Oh, it's really not a big deal. I wasn't sad at all—it's not like I was really all that pregnant." I smiled and told her I was glad she was doing okay, then went to my car and cried behind the steering wheel.

Here's the thing—I believe there are many women for whom a miscarriage may not hit as hard as it did for me. But I don't believe this is always, or even often, the case. I think we've been told so often that it's not a big deal, to brush it off, to try again, that we've denied grieving mothers the time and space they need to truly heal. Now it's simply the expectation that expecting parents will get over losses quickly and move on. One by one, we deny our emotions and, in doing so, block our ability to extend empathy to others.

I've even done it myself. In my first book, I wrote, "When the doctors finally told us that it wasn't possible for us to have children, I was completely devastated. My heart was broken as my dreams of motherhood fell and shattered at my feet. I silently lashed out at God, at friends, and at myself. I felt like an utter failure."[2]

That description is entirely accurate. It is a true, deep down, honest reflection of my heart. But those aren't the words I wrote in my very first draft. In the first draft, I wrote, "When doctors finally told us that it wasn't possible for us to have children, I threw a spiritual and physical fit that would put any toddler to shame." The words never made it out of the proposal stage of the book because a wise and kind editor inserted a note next to my description: "Finding out you can't have biological children is devastating. Make sure you don't downplay your emotions by comparing this chapter of your life to a toddler having a temper tantrum. It is so much more than that, but if you downplay it, it comes across as you trying to make light of a difficult trial and it doesn't work here." Her note made me feel loved and seen. She was right. I was distancing myself from my true feelings, and how might that have impacted the reader?

What if a woman in the throes of infertility picked up my book and read my failure to honor my true feelings? How would it have impacted her to read that I considered grief over the inability to conceive nothing more than childish behavior? She'd likely (and rightfully) want to throw the book across the room. When we deny our emotions and dismiss our feelings, we shut down our access to empathy. Then, instead of offering neighborly love, we pour salt in open wounds.

If we are brave enough to honor our emotions, they can point us toward our hurting neighbors and help us to love them well. When we're honest, our feelings can show us what's missing in our neighborhood and where a need might be waiting that only we can fill. A world without emotions is a world without grace and compassion. A world without feelings is a world without understanding and care. I don't really want to live in that world.

Even if it's mocked, even if it hurts, and even if it's hard, let's choose empathy over apathy and honesty over masks. Big feelings lead to big love.

# EIGHT

# SCARLET LETTERS AND STRINGS OF PEARLS

*Vulnerability is the birthplace of love, belonging, joy, courage, empathy, and creativity. It is the source of hope, empathy, accountability, and authenticity.*
BRENÉ BROWN, *DARING GREATLY*

I was ten years old when I started having seizures. My first seizure came on a Tuesday night in October. My father had been away, though I don't remember where because, as an active member of the military, he was often away. My mother had left my older sister and me at home while she and our toddler brother went to the airport or the navy base to pick up my dad.

I remember playing Barbies on the floor until I got sleepy and climbed up to my bed—the top bunk. My dad came in at some point to say goodnight, but I had trouble waking up to greet him. He gently teased me about how tired I was.

I remember waking up on the bedroom floor with the lights shining brightly overhead, Dad's finger jammed in my mouth, and his voice screaming something to my mom about an ambulance. Then the paramedics wheeled a stretcher into our small bedroom and lifted me onto it. As I was wheeled out of our home, I caught sight of two neighbors watching from their yard. At the hospital, a nurse gave me an ice pack for my swollen and bruised bottom lip—evidently I had viciously chewed it during the seizure. She also offered an ice pack to my dad for his finger—the one he'd jammed in my mouth to keep me from swallowing my tongue. Evidently I'd chewed it to bits too.

I remember leaving the hospital in my nightgown, perched happily on my dad's shoulders as he cracked jokes and marched us out to the car. I talked to my Pap on the phone the next day and tried to tell him what had happened, but I had to ask my dad, "What's that thing I had called?" I couldn't remember the word *seizure*.

I remember my first CT scan and EEG, though they would be far from the last. During my first MRI, Dad stayed in the room and held my big toe the entire time so I wouldn't feel too frightened and alone.

I remember every single one of my neurologists, from San Diego to Washington D.C. to Norfolk.

I remember the blood draws and waiting in line to check out from the naval hospital after an afternoon of lab work. As I stood next to my father, black dots swirled in front of me and turned into a tunnel. I woke up on a table in an exam room with a giant Pink Panther attached to the light above me. That was the first time I fainted. Dad took me to McDonald's for a chocolate milkshake afterward. He told me it was for being so brave, but I bet he wanted to give me a boost of sugar too. It became a tradition we carried on throughout the years—any time I had to go to the doctor for exams or lab work or tests, we'd get a milkshake on the way home. I felt special because we had created a little tradition.

I remember my allergic reactions to seizure medications— the rash that covered my body, the nausea, the headaches, the confusion. One day I overheard my mom on the phone with my neurologist describing how I'd shattered a jar of pickles at the grocery store and not even noticed. "Something isn't right," she said. "She isn't herself. She's spaced out and zombie-like." I wondered then if I was going to die.

And then there are the memories that are more painful than these.

I will never forget how hard it was to navigate my life at school as an epileptic. I didn't have words for it at the time, but looking back, I realize I wanted to share the burden of it all with my friends. I wanted them to know what I was going through because it was hard, and I wanted them to really know me and support me. What I didn't yet understand but would soon discover is that not all school acquaintances are true friends—heck, not all "friends" are true friends.

One day a group of us girls were talking in the back of our fifth-grade classroom, and I decided to tell them I'd been having seizures. The group grew quiet and uncomfortable at first, and then a girl named Dana with short brown hair started laughing.

"You have seizures?!" Her voice grew loud, and my face turned red.

"My *dog* has seizures! You're like my dog!" She laughed hysterically, and the other girls joined her. For the rest of the year, any time I passed her on the playground or in the cafeteria, Dana barked at me while her friends giggled beside her.

When we moved away a year later, I was very cautious about who I shared myself with at my new school. I learned that once you share something, you can't put that particular genie back in the bottle. I learned to hide my hard.

I can't presume to know why others hide their hard, but I certainly know why I do. I can close my eyes and remember exactly how it felt when Dana laughed and barked at me, and I never want to experience that again. I still long for the love and support of my friends when life gets rough, but I struggle to get past my fear of their response. *What if they judge me? What if they laugh and point and use my pain against me? What if I have done something or not done something to deserve this, and they blame me? What if they don't care?* I know I'm not the only one who hesitates to reach out for support. Perhaps all of us have memories that make us pause before we reach for the phone or tap a shoulder. We fear having another experience of judgment, ridicule, or indifference. We fear the other person may not be trustworthy.

And yet, it is these very fears that have the potential to lead us closer to loving well. We can become the trustworthy persons we long for others to be when they are hurting. That's how we love our neighbors with empathy and grace when they choose to open up to us. When someone raises a hand and tenderly shares their hard, how do we respond? Do we meet the vulnerability of others with outstretched arms, or a grand inquisition and cold platitudes? When someone trusts us enough to let us in, it is imperative that we recognize we are being offered a gift. Someone trusts us with a piece of their story—a piece of themselves—and we must prove ourselves trustworthy in response.

In Matthew 25, Jesus tells his followers a parable about a man who leaves his property in the care of three servants while he goes on a trip. To the first servant he gives five talents, the second servant gets two, and the third servant receives just one. The man trusts his servants to invest his money wisely, and the first two servants do so. When the man returns and asks his servants for an accounting, the first two have doubled their investments. Unfortunately, the third servant did absolutely nothing with what he'd been given. He simply buried his talent in the ground and waited for his boss to return. The boss, who had rewarded the first two servants, is furious. He throws out the third servant and gives his one talent to the first trustworthy servant.

The parable is a harsh warning about the dangers of wasting whatever it is God has entrusted to us. But it can also teach us something about how to be wise when someone entrusts us with a piece of their story. Imagine with me . . .

A woman is going through a hard season of life. She's trying to keep her head above water, but most days she feels like she's drowning. She's afraid and vulnerable, but she chooses to entrust her story to three friends. First Friend listens as the woman talks, holds her hand while she cries, and hugs her tightly when the words stop. A few days later, the woman sends a text, "Want to meet for coffee on Tuesday morning?" As they sit over coffee, First Friend asks how things are going. She listens and cares. She offers to babysit the kids for an afternoon. That first coffee turns into a weekly coffee. First Friend takes the gift of the woman's story and invests it in their friendship.

Second Friend responds similarly to the first. She listens and cares. Her life isn't set up to allow for weekly coffee talks and babysitting, but she offers what she can. About once a week, she sends encouraging texts to let the woman know she's thinking about her and to ask how she's doing. Every once in a while, she leaves surprise treats in the woman's mailbox—cookies, a kind note, little gifts to make her smile. These small gestures lift the woman's spirit and always seem to come at just the right moment. The woman knows she can trust Second Friend.

Third Friend initially appears to receive the gift of the woman's vulnerability well. She listens and seems to care when they get together, and they part with a hug. But that's it. She never checks back in. When she sees the woman at the store or church or the playground, she acts as if everything is fine and normal . . . as if the woman had never opened up and shared at all. The woman is confused and hurt and a little angry. She wishes she'd never opened up to Third Friend and vows not to trust her again.

I could take some liberties with the parable and add

another character, Fourth Friend. Perhaps she's the one who receives the woman's story with skepticism and judgment. Instead of a shoulder to cry on, she offers a barrage of questions. *What choices did you make to create this situation? Didn't you see it coming? How could you have prevented it?* Her friendship is conditional. Fourth Friend makes it clear that she'll only help if the woman does things differently. Instead of feeling loved and supported, the woman walks away feeling ashamed.

And maybe there is yet another: Fifth Friend. She sits with the woman and urges her to continue sharing. She nods and listens and wants the woman to go even deeper. "Tell me everything," she says. "I'm here for you!" She steeps a pot of tea and gives the woman a reassuring pat on the knee every now and then. But when all the juicy details are spilled and the woman walks out the door, Fifth Friend jumps on the phone to share the news.

I've had a few encounters with Fifth Friend myself. I've watched as gossip flows through the church under the guise of "prayer chains." It's couched in Christianese: "Friends, we need to be praying for so-and-so because I just heard her husband is having an affair, and here's what happened." Fifth Friend in my small group has asked me to share more details about my life than I was comfortable sharing because, "It will help us know how to pray for you." And it wasn't long until I discovered that my pain, my life, my story had been shared widely beyond the small group.

The sad truth is, I see myself in all of these characters, and perhaps you do too. I've been the woman who is broken by tragedy and bending under the weight of life. I've been the friend who fails to support others when they trust me with their story. I've judged when I should have loved, and I've gossiped when I should have prayed. And then there are, mercifully, times when I have gotten it right and loved unconditionally with my words and deeds.

A well-known pastor and theologian once posted on Twitter, "Everyone says they want community and friendship. But mention accountability or commitment to people, and they run the other way." I understand what this pastor may have meant, but I have to admit that his words give me pause. In fact, they make my internal alarm bells scream like wailing sirens.

There are times in Christian circles when "accountability" is simply spiritualized cover for refusing to respect a person's boundaries and pressuring them to share more than they want. "Commitment" can also be confused with staying in an abusive environment or allowing oneself to be trampled. Perhaps if people want community and friendship but are running away from church, it says less about their disdain for accountability and commitment and more about the failure of those in the church to be a trustworthy community of friends.

When people hesitate to commit, or to be vulnerable about struggles in a way that would invite accountability and support, the problem may not be with them alone. Perhaps we need to look inside and ask ourselves why we haven't yet been deemed trustworthy. Have *we* committed to *them*? Have we been consistent in pursuing friendship? Have we been open and vulnerable ourselves, sharing our own struggles and pain? When someone doesn't want to jump in the center of the trust circle, chances are it's because there's a break in the chain somewhere. When people are running away from us, we have to at least consider that they have been hurt and we haven't yet proven ourselves worthy of their trust.

※

One of my favorite childhood movies is *Seven Brides for Seven Brothers*. Watching it as an adult, I see several highly problematic themes in this 1954 classic, staring Jane Powell and Howard Keel. But as a young girl, I delighted in the music and dancing and comedy and romance. I especially loved how Milly, the first bride, whipped a house full of seven rowdy men into shape and made a mountain man bachelor pad into a cozy cabin in the woods. I've watched the film a couple dozen times, so I have most of the lines memorized. As I've thought about what holds us back from reaching out for support in tough times, the scene from Milly's first night in the mountains springs to mind.

Milly has just married the oldest of seven brothers earlier in the day and then worked hard to cook all of them a large dinner. Instead of sitting politely, thanking her for the meal, and eating it with even a shred of manners, the brothers devour the meal with their hands and get into an argument that turns into a massive food fight. In anger, she runs up to the room she'll share with her new husband and grabs her Bible from the bedside table. Quickly turning the pages, she reads aloud Matthew 7:6: "Give not that which is holy unto the dogs, neither cast ye your pearls before swine, lest they trample them under their feet, and turn again and rend you" (KJV).

That verse halts me in my tracks. Don't give what is precious to just anyone, because there are people out there who will take your pearls and stomp on them—then turn around and use them to attack you.

I'm not aware of anyone in my circle of people who would purposely trample me, but I know this happens. It's hard not to wonder how many people out there find themselves surrounded by once trusted friends who turned around and used their pain against them. How many people have reached out for help only to find their hand swatted away, or their news spread throughout the community rumor mill? How many people have opened their hearts and arms, hoping for a hug, and instead been stamped with a scarlet letter of shame? How many little girls hold in their hearts their version of being barked at on the fifth-grade playground? Perhaps we have people all around us who have been conditioned to hold back. Perhaps we are one of them.

❧

Last year, I completed a day of friend and family training at a rehabilitation center. I spent some time with Heather, an addiction counselor, who described how the center helps people who are struggling to overcome drug and alcohol addiction. She herself is a recovering alcoholic and has been sober for over twenty years. She told me that she still attends an AA meeting every three days. "It's my insurance policy," she said.

She went on to share more about AA, NA, and Al-Anon, and the importance of accountability and support in recovery. It was an eye-opening day, and one that I wish could be part of every high school and college curriculum—a requirement for graduation. My compassion widened for the people I love who have been stuck in the cycle of addiction.

I was also able to sit in on an Al-Anon meeting and witness the power of sitting together, validating the story of another, and sharing my own. One by one, we went around the circle and shared. No two stories were the same, and I couldn't relate to the experiences of a single other person in that room. But when the circle ended with me and as I nervously began to speak, I saw nothing but compassion and care in the faces watching me. Everyone's pain was unique, but we were sitting together and telling it. I held their stories and they held mine with tender, gentle hands. No one judged anyone else, and no one tried to fix anyone else. I could understand why Heather made sure she was sitting in an AA meeting every three days more than twenty years into her sobriety. The vulnerability, acceptance, and connection found there was powerful. Titles were left at the door as everyone sat down with simply their true, broken selves. It was a meaningful experience.

After the meeting, I couldn't help but wish there were a version of Al-Anon or AA for regular life—call it HA, Humans Anonymous. But really what I was wishing is that the church would follow a similar model. That small groups left power hierarchies at the door and the pastor's wife and deacons were just as open and vulnerable as the rest of us are pressed to be. We could give people permission to be sad and scared and lonely, and we could do it together. We could look to our left and to our right and say, "I'm hurting and you're hurting, and I don't always understand your pain and you might not get mine, but we can still sit together. Stay and tell me your story, and I'll tell you mine. Maybe we'll cry. I promise I won't try to fix you and I won't judge you; I just want to sit with you. You can trust me with your story."

But this isn't something most of us have figured out how to do that well.

There are some who glorify vulnerability and transparency to an unhealthy degree. They urge others to show their true selves—all their mess. In some Christian circles, the message for those struggling with sin is, "Confess! There's freedom in the light!" Sin and suffering are conflated, and we assume authenticity requires exposure: "Show us your dirty laundry, so we know you're human—anything less is fake!" But what isn't considered is that perhaps those who hesitate to confess or expose themselves in such ways aren't being fake or deceitful. Perhaps they are protecting broken hearts.

I thought of this recently when I read a heartbreaking essay—soon to be expanded into a book—by writer, musician, and activist Andre Henry. It is an open letter to all the friends he couldn't keep. Specifically, all the white friends he, as a black man, had to let go. He describes how he had tried to share his experience as a black man in America. He offered his pain and vulnerability as a gift, and it was rejected—not just by some but by many, and not just once but repeatedly.

I didn't block any of you because of hate. I don't hate you. I love you. I blocked you because you showed no empathy.

Not one time, did any of you reach out to me and say, "Help me understand."

Not one of you ever called me to ask, "Are you okay?"

It was only, "Were you this upset at Obama?" "Are you actually likely to be racially attacked?" "Prove to me that racism is a thing!" "Tell me, Andre! What sins of my ancestors should I atone for!"

You mocked me, even as I said, "I understand why you might feel like racism isn't a thing, but . . ."

I learned again. I learned that speaking softly to you doesn't matter. Because this isn't about how I say it. This is about what I'm saying.

You call me angry as though I have no reason to be.

You say I'm a troublemaker as though there's not already trouble around me.

You show no urgency to care for us. You're looking for reasons not to.

I can't bear to see you, knowing how little you care about me, and knowing how deeply I believed that you loved me. I can't watch your faces scroll across my Facebook feed and remember the smug tones, the blank faces, and the smart remarks you served me when I told you how much it hurts sometimes to be black in this country.[1]

In a perfect world, we could be totally transparent. In a perfect world, we'd trade our scarlet letters for strings of pearls and wear them proudly without fear they'd be torn from our necks and trampled on. In a perfect world, we could share our deepest, darkest fears and pain and struggles. We could be open about the sins we wrestle with and the pain we carry without worrying that they would be splashed across the church prayer chain or buzzed around the school playground. We wouldn't be shunned or judged or treated with anything other than tenderness, love, compassion, and friendship.

We don't live in a perfect world, but we are commanded to love our neighbor as ourselves in the broken world we're navigating. We must respond with empathy when someone trusts us with their broken heart. It is a gift that keeps on giving, because, as others trust us with their stories, we learn and grow in ways that increase our empathy and allow us to love our neighbors more with each passing day.

# STRANGERS ARE JUST NEIGHBORS WE HAVEN'T MET YET

All good people agree,
And all good people say,
All nice people, like Us, are We
And every one else is They:
But if you cross over the sea,
Instead of over the way,
You may end by (think of it!) looking on We
As only a sort of They!
RUDYARD KIPLING, "WE AND THEY," *DEBITS AND CREDITS*

T hey don't know each other!" The exclamation rang from the back seat of our minivan. My son had watched two of his friends get into a yelling and kicking match at Vacation Bible School the week before. Mareto knew these two friends from different contexts—one from the neighborhood and the other from his sister's preschool—but these two friends had never met each other. When they did meet, as can happen with preschoolers, they got into a squabble over something silly. Mareto was upset and trying to understand. When I asked why the kids were fighting, his response was both simple and profound: *they don't know each other.*

My son believes children fight because they don't know each other. If they actually got to know each other, they would get along and become friends. I think he's on to something. When I look at the world today, I see so much fear and misunderstanding. I see it in the choices we make and the way we build our lives: our social circles, churches, schools, and neighborhoods. Human beings naturally gravitate toward similarity rather than difference. We tend to seek out those who are like us in a variety of ways. The challenge this poses in our current culture is that our affinity for similarity has led to polarization and, subsequently, fear. It's the fear of others that causes us to act in ways that are apathetic or even hateful rather than loving. That fear is often because we simply don't know each other. As a result, our social fabric—locally and globally—is unraveling.

My son's exclamation often echoes in my mind when I see things play out in my own community and in the news. What if, instead of dehumanizing each other—creating caricatures and stereotypes—we spent time together and created friendships? Perhaps we'd see that different isn't bad and strangers are simply neighbors we haven't met yet.

I live in a suburban neighborhood in a small city that was founded the year after the Declaration of Independence was signed. We bought our home with our children and our dog in mind—we wanted enough rooms to hold our family and enough yard to hold our dog. It helped that the kitchen had white cabinets and the street was quiet, with a playground three houses down from us. It would be fair to say that most of the people on our street share the same economic class as us. To my knowledge, no one has gone to bed hungry, had their water or heat cut off, been evicted, or forced to foreclose on their home. Everyone around us seems comfortable. The neighborhood a couple blocks away tells a different story, but it would be easy to assume that my street is standard.

Many of our friends are college graduates like us—a side effect of living in a tiny town that is home to two colleges and being married to a man who works at one of them. I've made most of my friends at the playground where I take my kids after school or at the city pool on summer afternoons. Most of my friends are moms, like me, with young children. We gather in the same spaces and find each other like moths drawn to porch lights. Connecting is easy, almost effortless, because of our shared experiences. We are mostly white, female, middle-class. Welcome to my bubble.

It would be easy to view anyone outside my bubble as strange, other, and frightening. It would be easy, but it would be wrong.

Research has shown that our empathy is diminished to the point of being virtually absent when the suffering person is a member of a different social, racial, or cultural group.[1]

Because of our bubble-induced blind spots, we simply can't see people whose experience differs from our own.

If we want to love our neighbors, we have to break out of our bubbles. And perhaps nothing is better at bursting bubbles than face-to-face interaction. When we leave our comfort zones, we find a whole new world waiting for us—full of beauty, heartbreak, hope, pain, love, loss, and everything that makes all of us human. We find that we aren't as different as we once feared and that the differences we do have make life more beautiful and interesting and fun.

There can be great joy in popping the bubbles we've made of our lives. Just as my kids run through the grass on a summer evening and shriek with delight as they chase the bubbles I've blown through the Dollar Tree plastic wand, we can run toward each other and reach out our arms until our bubbles burst. There is pleasure and joy and hope in spending time with people who aren't just like us. And there is something else too—empowerment.

Not long ago, I had the honor of attending a lecture given by Rev. Dr. William Barber II. Rev. Barber has spent his life in service to others, and in particular he has championed the poor. He is co-chair of the new Poor People's Campaign, the first having been started in 1968 by Martin Luther King Jr. He travels the country sharing his hope for a better tomorrow. I was overjoyed when I learned he was coming to our small community, and the event was open to the public. I wrote the date and time in my calendar and then brought my entire family to hear him speak.

There were many quote-worthy statements in his lecture, but one continuing thread stuck out to me more than anything else. It started when he paraphrased a portion of the speech given by Dr. King at the conclusion of the 1965 Selma-to-Montgomery marches. Rev. Barber explained that whenever the black people and the poor white masses in the South began to unite in their efforts to build a society based on justice and plenty and brotherhood, someone—those in positions of economic and social power—used division to keep them from seeing one another.[2] This theme wove its way throughout Rev. Barber's lecture—that division is a tool used to perpetuate economic and social systems that benefit those in power.

The powers that be knew, and feared, the greater power of unity—the power of people coming together. The power is in the empathy that grows out of living with one another and seeing the humanity in each of us. The power is in the care and compassion and love that comes with the unknown becoming known, the strange becoming ordinary, suspicion giving way to comfort, and fear falling away to form friendship. When we use our resources to build bridges instead of bubbles, everybody—instead of just a few somebodies—gets richer in the things that really matter.

Our family has a few members who live with various disabilities. Some are more pronounced than others, which means our day-to-day lives—both the joys and the struggles—can look different from most of the families around us. Friendships can be particularly difficult for one of my children as the differences with peers become more obvious with age. It's not always cruelty that keeps potential friends at bay, but confusion and perhaps a bit of fear.

John and I spoke to a counselor about it. My temptation was to cry and rage and vilify the children who were not including mine. But John took a more introspective approach as he remembered being in grade school and feeling uncertain about playing with an intellectually disabled child. He explained that he didn't know if they would have anything in common or anything to talk about. He thought it would be awkward and uncomfortable, but then he spent some time with that child, and they had fun together. In fact, the more time they spent together, the more fun they had and the closer friends they became.

There are numerous studies that show what we have personally experienced: disabled children have lower rates of acceptance and companionship with their peers. But the effort required to connect cannot fall completely on the shoulders of disabled individuals. Often, disabled children are left out because group activities are geared toward those without disabilities. If all the second-grade boys play a game of pickup soccer each day at recess, but one of the boys lacks the executive functioning to navigate the rules and speed of the game and finds himself yelled at and sidelined day after day, is the lack of connection his fault? Maybe the third-graders all run out to play tag, but a little girl with gross motor delays finds herself constantly "it" because the other kids know she can't run and react quickly enough to catch them. So the little girl retreats to a tunnel in the playground equipment to hide her tears. Is her isolation her fault? The peers in these scenarios aren't trying to be mean; they simply don't understand. But if we separate disabled children from the others, the world doesn't become a more accessible place. Inclusion doesn't happen naturally; it has to be taught and fought for.

A few years ago, a local high schooler named Ella recognized a need for more connection between neurotypical students and those with disabilities. She responded by starting a nonprofit called Project Connection that "promotes acceptance and connection between high schoolers in the area and kids with disabilities, ESL children, refugees, or the siblings of a child with a disability."[3] Project Connection holds monthly events for teens and their "buddies" that help create bonds using art, music, games, and a host of other activities. When I asked her about it, here is how Ella described her motivation for creating Project Connection:

> I am originally from Charlotte, North Carolina, and I spent the first fifteen years of my life there. Charlotte is a big, diverse, growing city, so I grew up meeting people from all sorts of backgrounds. In the eighth grade, I joined a nonprofit in Charlotte called Playing for Others. One aspect of their programming is a buddy program between students in eighth to twelfth grades and kiddos with special needs. It was by far my favorite part of the programming in PFO, and I was devastated when my family told me we were moving.
>
> After settling in Lexington, Virginia, I immediately noticed some differences between it and Charlotte. A lot more people look like me and have similar backgrounds to me. There is less visible diversity, and it just felt so

much more excluded, sheltered, and closed off. I also noticed that, at least in the high school, there was no specialized program that connected "typical" students with students with disabilities. Thinking back to my passion for the buddy programming in PFO, I knew I wanted to start something similar.

Project Connection started off exactly the same as PFO's buddy programming—partnerships between teens and kids with special needs. While many of our buddy trios and our program aspects are still this way and that is our major focus, PC has also expanded to be a safe space where diversity and differences are celebrated. We have three C's in PC—Compassion, Community, and Connection.

After experiencing the differences between big-city Charlotte and small-town Lexington, I felt that there was a need for those components to be addressed in our town—and specifically with the young people. Neither big-city Charlotte or small-town Lexington are better than the other, and there are pros and cons of both! But what makes PC so special and needed in a community like Lexington is that we are a close-knit group of citizens—most people know each other in the city and county. So why not establish a basis of being compassionate toward one other, no matter our physical, developmental, or internal differences? Why not make the community more connected and accepting? That's what PC aims to do each and every day, and that is the main reason why I started PC and why I believe it is continuing with such success.

As much as I love what Project Connection is about, I was resistant when first approached about my children participating. Trust a group of teenagers with my precious babies? *Are you kidding me?!* But Ella was persistent, and as I began to learn more about the teens involved and the careful planning and execution of their events, I grew more comfortable. It took about a year, but I eventually signed up the kids, they were matched with their teen buddies, and I dropped them off at their first event—a holiday themed party. That was three years ago, and since that time, I've seen the vision of Project Connection come to life before my eyes.

Not only are these teenagers getting to know children of varying backgrounds and abilities, but my kids are spending time with teens who are kind and fun and smart and silly. They have a group of role models to look up to who love pouring back into our lives. Once a month John and I get two hours on a Saturday afternoon to go out for coffee, take a walk, or simply sit and take a deep breath. I've seen how amazing the next generation is. I've seen their passion and drive, their energy, vision, and hope. It may seem like a small thing, just two hours once a month, but I believe it also has a ripple effect that expands far beyond those Saturday events.

The next time one of those teens sees a person in a wheelchair, he won't feel awkward and nervous about how to speak to them, because he will have spent plenty of time with people who use a wheelchair. If one of those teens grows up to become a pediatrician, she'll have extra grace and empathy for children showing signs of autism—even better, she'll know what signs to look for. And when I'm at the grocery store or movie theater or gas station and see a group of teenagers laughing and causing a ruckus, I no longer roll my eyes at their immaturity. Instead, I smile at their joy and energy and carefree spirit. I've seen firsthand how those things can be directed in amazing ways. This is the powerful ripple effect that happens when strangers become neighbors.

When we get to know each other, when we spend time together face-to-face, we learn about the things that might have previously scared us off or confused us. And as cliché as it sounds, knowledge is power. It shines a light in the shadows. There can be difficult barriers to overcome in drawing near to one another, but we have to try.

On our third trip to Ethiopia, John and I seemed to catch the same taxi driver nearly every time we left our hotel. He was kind and chatty, so we got to know him fairly well during our week in Addis Ababa. During one ride through the city, we got to talking about languages, and I asked if he'd learned English in school as a child. It turns out, he'd taught himself to speak English as an adult because he wanted to be able to converse with tourists. "People are so interesting," he said, "I want to be able to talk to them!" We then learned that he also spoke a moderate amount of Spanish and German and was currently teaching himself to speak Chinese! He held up a well-worn Chinese-Amharic dictionary, and my jaw dropped. "I'm getting pretty good!" he told us. "I can have very basic conversations with the businessmen I meet from China."

I have to confess, I felt about two inches tall.

It wasn't just that he spoke so many different languages and was completely self-taught that amazed me. It was his reason for learning to speak so many languages: he wanted to get to know people. The only people I have real friendships with are the ones who speak English. Aside from a couple of years studying Spanish in high school and two years of French in college, I'd never given learning another language a second thought. Whom have I missed out on because I can't communicate with them? How could I have grown up less than an hour's drive from Mexico and never learned to speak Spanish? The town I live in now has a fairly large Latinx population, and for years it never even occurred to me to learn their language.

As much as I admired our taxi driver in Ethiopia, it has been my daughter who has inspired change in me. In her final year of preschool, she had a warm and loving teacher from Colombia. Her teacher often spoke both English and Spanish in the classroom in order to include a little boy who only spoke Spanish. Arsema delighted in listening to her teacher move back and forth between each language and came home showing off different words she'd learned. Once she even went home from school with her teacher and helped her make lunch and water her garden while we had a doctor appointment with Mareto. She came home as besotted as ever, begging us to teach her to speak Spanish. "We'll figure it out," I promised her, and slowly we are. I signed up the kids for Spanish club and downloaded an app for myself. I may be slow (gosh, I wish I'd taken it more seriously in my youth), but I'm learning because I want to be able to know and love my neighbors.

I can't help but smile wondering what heaven will be like. The Bible assures us that the kingdom of God includes people "from every nation, from all tribes and peoples and languages" (Revelation 7:9). Will we all speak one language or every language? I can't wait to find out. How could we let things such as language, culture, and borders keep us from the joy of knowing one another on earth when heaven itself is filled with such beautiful diversity?

One of my dearest friends is a woman from Afghanistan who moved to the United States as a young adult and married a man my husband went to college with. After living on the same street for many years, we now live on opposite ends of the county, but we work together at a local bakery and see each other any weekend our schedules allow us to.

Throughout our friendship she's taught me more than she probably realizes. We spend equal amounts of time talking about the cultural differences between Afghanistan and America as we do recounting our favorite episodes of *Friends* and laughing ourselves silly. I've learned what it was like to grow up under the Taliban and the challenges faced by girls seeking education in that environment. She's listened to me reminisce about growing up in California and the culture shock of being transplanted to Virginia (though it's laughably mild compared to the culture shock she's experienced).

She's taught me how to make naan, though I can never get mine to turn out as well as hers does, and I bake birthday cakes for her kids. Each time I leave her presence, I walk away richer for it.

When the news reports that bombs have exploded in Kabul, I no longer change the channel but grieve the destruction of my friend's hometown and the loss of her former neighbors. When refugees are vilified in the news or in conversation, I am resolute in my defense of them. When racist comments are made about people of Middle Eastern descent, it stings, and I know how ignorant and ridiculous xenophobia is. This is the power of coming together—it creates friendships that erase the illusion of us versus them.

When we step out of our bubbles and share our experiences, food, culture, histories, hopes, and dreams, it becomes obvious—there is no *them*, there is only *us*. This can be shown in the little things like breaking naan together, visiting churches outside your denomination, and inviting the lonely kid over after school. And it's in the big things like learning a new language or starting a nonprofit. When we choose togetherness, when we scale walls and cross borders, we are reminded that we are all human and all deserving of second chances, friendship, and love. The beautiful side effect of coming together is the cultivation of empathy and seeing strangers become neighbors.

TEN

# THE NEXT RIGHT THING

A broken heart is not the end of anything. It's the
beginning of everything.
GLENNON DOYLE, MOMASTERY.COM

It was a Sunday evening late last fall and the night was
clear but cold. I parked my van on the quiet, dark street
and hurried to the other side. I descended old stone steps
on the side of a church built in the nineteenth century and
entered a basement meeting room. Inside, a group of about
ten people sat around a long rectangular table—some faces
were familiar, but most were not. I nervously took a seat
at the corner end of the table and waited for the meeting
to start.

Stepping into new situations without a clear picture of
how things will go is not my forte. I hadn't told anyone I was
coming to this meeting, and no one had invited me. I just saw

116

an announcement on Facebook that it was open to the public and decided to show up. I fidgeted in my seat, my hands wrapped around a thermos of hot soup. In my rush to make sure the kids were fed before I left for the evening, I hadn't had time to eat myself. I took a swig of broth and winced as it burned the roof of my mouth. Swallowing quickly, I shifted uncomfortably and began to regret coming at all.

It would have been so much easier to stay home and have a quiet evening with my family. I could have gotten a head start on packing school lunches and setting out outfits for the next morning. Maybe we would have played a board game. But I remembered why I was sitting in a church basement with a group of people who were mostly strangers. It all started with a promise I'd made a few weeks earlier.

My kids had come home from school with questions about things they'd heard that day about Rosa Parks and Martin Luther King Jr. "They went to jail!" Mareto exclaimed with wide eyes. The information wasn't new, but he seemed to want me to understand what a big deal that was. Another little boy in class had asked about the Civil War, and my kids had more questions about slavery. We sat in the driveway for the better part of an hour talking through many things, including white supremacy.

They struggled to pronounce "supremacy." It was a word that got jumbled and turned around in their minds and came out awkward, twisted, and uncomfortable—a hissing onomatopoeia. We discussed the ways white supremacy continues to affect the world we live in today, and I stressed that no matter what they might hear from anyone else, it is always bad and always wrong.

"It's not fair." The sad sentence came from the back seat with a heaviness that broke my heart. I turned and held their hands tightly as I said as clearly and strongly as I could, "It's *not* fair. I want you to know that I will always fight against white supremacy. I will do all I can to stop it. I promise I will never stop trying to make the world fair for you."

Later that night, when the kids were tucked into bed and the house was quiet, I thought about my promise. I meant it, but at the same time I wondered what fulfilling it would look like—and if I was living up to it yet. I had to be honest and admit I wasn't. I hadn't promised them that I would sit at home and hate racism in all its forms; I had promised them that I would invest my time in doing the work to upend racism. I needed to follow through.

In recent months I had picked up a habit of avoidance. I would see a news story about the violent death of a black teenager and immediately click away—I couldn't tolerate the terror that rose up in me as my son's face flashed to the forefront of my mind. I found it unbearable to hear news stories about little black girls whose natural hair had been deemed inappropriate for school. One had her braids cut off by a teacher and another was expelled. My eyes welled with tears as I thought about Saturday evenings spent with my daughter's head propped up by my knees, an assortment of combs and creams by my side, and the feel of her soft curls sliding through my fingers as I braid and twist them. I thought about her wide smile each time she looks in the mirror when we finish her weekly 'do. Proudly, she turns her head left and right as she examines my work, and I ask, "Do you like it?" She nods and grins—pleased with her braids, twists, Bantu knots, or wash-n-go curls. The thought of someone making her feel less-than because of the way the hair grows out of her head makes my stomach twist into knots tighter than the ones on her head. I don't even like it when people touch her hair out of admiration. The thought of someone taking scissors to her braids? Unbearable. So I click away—the story hurts too much.

Day after day, the news and social media bring a barrage of stories about how black children are treated harshly in schools and how black teens and adults suffer at the hands of the justice system or authorities in the workplace. Each story rubs my heart until it's raw and bleeding and feels like just too much, or so I tell myself. So I turn off the news; I click away; I close my eyes. I want to exist in my happy bubble of a home with my kids safe in my care. But my avoidance and fragility doesn't protect them from the world, nor does it help me to love my neighbors.

That's how I wound up in the church basement at the meeting held by our local anti-racism group. I chose to look more closely at what was breaking my heart and making my skin crawl. Instead of turning away from the things that rub my heart raw, I turned toward them. And as I sat at the table, listening to and learning from people who had been facing the pain of our community head-on, I felt a sense of purpose and renewed hope. Avoidance and apathy feed despair, but we find strength when we invest ourselves in helping where we hurt. And I have learned that bleeding hearts can be the strongest when we choose to do something about the cause of the wound.

If we have empathy for one another—if their pain breaks

our hearts and their joy makes us smile—but it never extends beyond the walls of our hearts, empathy has not become love. Empathy is the flashlight that guides us along the path toward loving our neighbors. When we begin to walk in another's shoes, we must ask ourselves, "Where are these shoes taking me?" Then we must be willing to follow where empathy leads, because empathy is only as effective—as loving—as the action it prompts us to take. Taking action requires courage and resolve, but it is always worth it to do the next right thing.

I have been afraid of so many things: the mental and emotional toll that justice work would take, the discrimination and dangers that await my children, the attacks and judgment from peers, and the list goes on. But these fears seem small and dim in the bright light of my children's future—in their hopes and dreams and potential. My fear is nearly extinguished by the light of the gospel and Christ's example of turning toward, rather than away from, the brokenness of the world.

Everywhere he went, Jesus encountered those who were hurting. Parents with dying children, the disabled who had been cast aside by society, the sick, the poor, the hated, the grieving. Day after day, town after town, each new place brought new stories of suffering. But instead of running away, instead of hiding at home, instead of closing his eyes and turning away, Jesus met each suffering person face-to-face. He didn't ignore the pain of life on earth while preaching about the kingdom of heaven. One of my favorites of these encounters is when Jesus meets a woman with an issue of blood. It is a short story, but one whose significance is indicated by the fact that three out of the four Gospels tell it.[1]

It happens as an interruption. Jesus is on his way somewhere else, to restore life to a local ruler's beloved daughter who has just died. Crowds surround him as he goes along the road and hidden among them is a woman who has been bleeding for twelve years. Both Mark and Luke note that she has spent all her money on doctors, and Mark indicates that she has suffered greatly at the hands of her physicians. We don't know exactly what her illness is, but it seems safe to assume she has a painful condition related to her menstrual cycle. Her suffering is compounded by the fact that her bleeding would have made her ceremonially unclean under Jewish law. This means she has likely lived in social and spiritual isolation for all the years of her illness. She is desperate but also full of faith. As she presses toward Jesus, she whispers to herself, *If I only touch his garments, I will be made well.* And then she does just that. Pushing through the crowds, she extends her hand until her fingertips reach the fringe of his garment. In that brush of finger to fabric, her body is healed.

Jesus stops immediately and turns to the crowd. "Who touched me?" he demands to know. In fear and trembling, the woman comes forward, and when she does, Jesus' gaze softens. He speaks tenderly to her, "Daughter, your faith has made you well; go in peace, and be healed of your disease" (Mark 5:34). Jesus is not angry, or bothered, or indifferent to her pain. He is patient and compassionate and willing to heal her. Even as he is on his way to help another hurting soul, he makes time for the suffering woman at his feet.

It doesn't matter how many times I read this short story, it always moves me to tears. When the woman is crouched on the ground, I see my own body in years past, bent over in crippling pain. When I read that she has spent all her money and suffered with many doctors, my thoughts flash to all the exam rooms, pharmacies, and operating rooms I've spent time in. I see the mounting stack of medical bills on the kitchen counter. I remember the years of suffering through my own monthly issue of blood when I suffered with endometriosis and was desperate to conceive. Seeing that Jesus was moved, not just emotionally but also moved to action, brings me such comfort and hope. It also fills me with purpose and instills in me a deep sense of responsibility to use the grace Jesus extended to me as a catalyst to love others.

Christ is our example of how to respond when our hearts break for others—we act. Beautiful things can happen when we let empathy propel us to action.

My friend Rachel's brother, Joshua, came to their family as a baby who had experienced extreme neglect and abuse in his birth family. His body was stiff and curled into itself—instinctive self-protection. With time and care and patience, he relaxed into his new home and family. But so much damage had been done to his heart and body and brain in those first few months of life that he never fully recovered.

Josh became addicted to drugs in his teenage years and

spent the rest of his life in and out of jail and rehabilitation centers. He had a strong network of support and people around him who loved him fiercely. He tried to fight his disease, but ultimately Josh succumbed to addiction and died young of a drug overdose.

Rachel describes her shock and grief the night her brother died as one long wail. On her refrigerator, a photograph held in place by a small magnet features a handsome young man in baggy jeans and a crisp white T-shirt. She smiles as she remembers that the picture had been taken while Josh was incarcerated. "He looks so good here!" she says. "He was clean and sober." Her love for her brother emanates from her eyes, her gestures, and her warm expression.

When the youngest of her three children entered preschool a few years ago, Rachel decided to return to work. As a nurse, Rachel considered several options, but her heart continued to be pulled toward the local county jail, so she filled out an application. She was quickly hired and began working the night shift a few times a week, administering medications and care to the inmates. It wasn't always easy—Rachel has her share of "war stories"—but when she talks about work, her face lights up.

Not long after she started working at the jail, I noticed she began to talk about her brother more often. He had been gone for several years, but she said she recognized him in the inmates she served. They weren't monsters, but good men—or boys—who had made some bad decisions. Some of them had known lives of awful abuse, and others had gotten caught up in a tough crowd, but all of them were really just scared and lonely. She treated them like the people she knew they were inside—human beings deserving of respect and love. "I see so much of Josh in these guys," she says. She treats each inmate the way she hopes someone would have treated her brother when he was incarcerated.

Rachel inspires me to love better. She could have chosen to work in a hospital or a nursing home, settings that wouldn't have been a continual reminder of the brother she lost far too soon. Instead, Rachel chose to turn toward her pain, allowing it to shape and soften her heart. Rachel allowed her heartbreak to cultivate empathy and then extended it to those who don't often receive empathy. Some days, she cries on the way home from work, but most days she leaves full of the joy that comes from following where empathy leads.

I don't have to look far to find other incredible people such as Rachel who have chosen to use their heartbreak to love others. My friend Emmy started an annual conference for women struggling with infertility after experiencing it herself. She bravely shares some of her most difficult moments on stage so others will know they aren't alone. When Lucy's seventeen-year-old son Jordan was shot and killed at a gas station, she began fighting for other families impacted by gun violence, and eventually ran for and won a seat in the United States House of Representatives.[2] When my friend Sarah's infant daughter died just four hours after her birth, she sought out ways to provide love and comfort to families with hospitalized children. She devoted hours to sewing tiny superhero capes to give to children living in hospice care.

These friends remind me, we are all braver and stronger than we realize, and we can't allow ourselves to squander our love by turning away from what breaks our hearts.

Last summer I spent hours at the community pool with my children. We had reached that magical place where both kids knew how to swim well enough for me to sit on a lounge chair and watch from a distance as they splashed and dove and jumped off the diving board. There was a steady rotation of friends for the kids to play with, as well as parents for me to enjoy adult conversation with.

One afternoon I was preoccupied by an article I had read that morning about children being separated from their parents as families sought asylum in our nation. More and more information was coming out about the conditions they were forced to endure, and the national outcry had reached fever pitch. It was weighing heavy on my heart, so I, thinking it might be helpful to process this together, raised the issue with an acquaintance at the pool. I was stunned when she said she didn't know what I was talking about.

This story had been front-page news for several weeks. How could she have missed it? Then she informed me that she had known something was going on, but she considered it too upsetting to know about, and so she had avoided the news altogether for over a month. In fact, she had stopped listening to the news on radio and television, checked only the email tab on her computer each day, and turned off all breaking-news notifications on her phone. She had put a lot of effort into protecting herself with detachment.

As shocked as I was that she was unaware of a crisis of such magnitude, a crisis that was harming human beings to such a degree that doctors classified it as a form of torture,

I also recognized a bit of myself in her response. I, too, feel the pull of detachment when things break my heart.

We tend to think of such detachment as a sort of safe neutrality. *We may not be doing anything to help*, we tell ourselves, *but at least we aren't part of the problem.* What we don't see is the damage we do—to ourselves and others—when we move through life wearing noise-canceling headphones. Nor do we see the waste of all the potential good we might do if we engaged.

What might happen if we instead chose to redirect all the effort we invest in detachment into flinging the doors of our hearts wide open? What might happen if we turned toward the crisis rather than away from it? Perhaps it would actually make our hearts stronger. Perhaps we could use our creativity to act with compassion and make a difference in someone else's life. We'll never know how we could have played a role in changing the world for the better if we aren't brave enough to open ourselves up to the things that scare us.

The lengths to which we'll go to distance ourselves from knowing too much about the suffering of others stems from a desire to protect ourselves from feeling the weight of this broken world. We're afraid we'll buckle beneath it. But our efforts do nothing to alleviate that suffering. I'm pretty sure that when a tree falls in the forest and no one is there to see or hear it, the tree still falls. Like it or not, when faced with heartbreak, we are always making a choice—to love or not to love.

Empathy is an invitation to love by choosing action. God has been shaping and preparing us our entire lives for this calling—to love our neighbor. Whether the neighbor is across the street or across the ocean, in the county jail or the nursing home, in the rehabilitation center or the maternity ward, at the border or the halls of congress, on the school campus or in the office cubicle—we make little choices to love or not love every day.

If we'll let it, the brokenness of the world can be the beginning of a beautiful journey. So, what's breaking your heart? What are you avoiding out of fear it might keep you up at night if you linger a little longer?

Is it hungry children?
Homelessness?
Those battling addiction?
The incarcerated?
Refugees?
Cancer patients?
Teenage mothers?
Gun violence?
Racial injustice?
The effects of climate change on our children?
Lack of access to clean water?
LGBTQ+ youth?
Victims of sexual assault?
Bereaved parents or spouses?
People struggling with mental illness?

Don't turn away from whatever it is that makes your heart break and your eyes well up with tears. Sit with it a little longer and see where your heart might lead you. Maybe you'll find yourself working at the county jail, volunteering at a rehabilitation center, or serving at a homeless shelter. Perhaps you'll sit fidgeting in a basement meeting room one evening and find yourself diving headfirst into activism. You might finally begin working for that law degree or find yourself demanding justice via megaphone on the steps of the Capitol building. Maybe you'll pass out hugs at a Pride Parade and find yourself locked in the embrace of a son or daughter who hasn't known the hug of a mother or father in years.

Where is empathy leading you to love? You might be scared, I know I am, but the next right thing is simply showing up—and we can do it.

# ELEVEN

# YOURS, MINE, OURS

This idea of selfishness as a virtue, as opposed to
generosity: That, to me, is unnatural.
JESSICA LANGE

On January 12, 2010, a catastrophic magnitude 7.0 earthquake hit the island nation of Haiti. Infrastructure was
destroyed, chaos and confusion hindered rescue efforts,
and over 230,000 lives were lost.[1] The reports coming out
of Haiti in the first few days were devastating. The utter
despair and staggering loss of life was impossible to turn
away from, and in the midst of it all we were preparing to
take a few dozen teenagers on a weekend church retreat.

My husband was a new youth pastor for children in
grades six through twelve. Each January the youth group
held their winter retreat at a facility just over an hour away.
It was our first year at this church, and we were still figuring

out how everything worked. John had secured a speaker for the weekend, reserved the cabin, and created a schedule. Evidently, it was tradition that the wives of the male youth leaders create the menu and prepare the meals during the retreat. Planning food for more than a few people was new to me, but I was trying to fit in and be helpful. Besides, I had help in the form of a few other wives who had done this before. We took the church credit card to Costco and filled our carts with food for the weekend.

Haiti was heavy on my mind as we loaded food and bottled water into our cars. I actually felt heartsick looking at all of it. This food wasn't going to help people who had lost everything; it was going to feed people who already had access to full pantries and refrigerators. The inequity of it all weighed on me like a load of bricks.

It was tension I battled with throughout that retreat weekend, and one with which I continue to struggle. I feel burdened by the enormous needs of the world and my own neighborhood. I am challenged when I read the words of Jesus: "Don't store up treasure here on earth. . . . Store your treasures in heaven" (Matthew 6:19–20 NLT). Then I think about our bursting closets, our well-stocked pantries, our two-car garages, and the ever-present drive to earn more money and climb the ladder of American success. How is it that we're somehow content for our ambition and, yes, our greed, to eclipse our mercy and our generosity? How have we allowed this to happen? Perhaps it's that we either don't know, or don't remember, what it feels like to be without.

A couple of years ago, our family went through an unexpected crisis that impacted every area of our lives, including our finances. After the worst had passed, I sat at my kitchen table with my best friend staring at a pile of bills, overdue notices, and upcoming expenses. Rachel listened, understood, and cracked jokes to help lighten the mood. Then we took a break and she drove with me to get the oil changed in my van. What started out as a quick and routine errand became another financial blow when the auto mechanic said, "You won't make it another week on those tires; all four are about to blow." I looked at my kids in the back seat, thought about those bills on the kitchen table, and felt utterly defeated.

I'd made a plan the week before—a plan for us to get back on our feet financially. It wouldn't happen overnight, but by the following spring or summer we would be okay. Now I was staring a $500 unplanned expense in the face, and I knew I couldn't cover it.

"Which two tires are the worst?" I asked. "I can replace those."

Rachel, who had overheard the whole exchange, immediately pulled out her wallet. "You need tires, Lauren."

I wasn't used to accepting help like that as an adult. I was used to being able to take care of all my needs on my own. Which is why I was somewhat surprised that I didn't feel embarrassed by Rachel's offer—I just felt loved.

Rachel was generous in a way that made it clear there were no strings attached. It was simply a natural extension of who she is and how she does life. *When you need something, I got you. When I need something, you got me.* It reminds me of a trust-building exercise I did once at a summer sports camp. A friend and I started off sitting back to back on the floor. We leaned on one another while pushing up with our legs and, before we knew it, we were both standing. But it only worked because we both leaned on each other with equal force. *I got you; you got me.*

I want to live a more generous life, and yet, the twenty-five dollars I just spent on a new swimsuit could have purchased a week of meals for a hungry child. The money I spent to attend a conference could have paid the deposit for a person struggling with addiction to check into a rehabilitation center. I glance through my cupboards and complain that there is "nothing good to eat." Which is really just another way of being picky and entitled. Even on a "bare" day, my cupboards hold enough food to feed my family just fine. My closet is full, but some Sunday mornings I complain that I have nothing to wear to church. What I really mean is that some of my nice clothes no longer fit in a perfectly flattering way, or that I want more options, or, more likely, that I'm bored with them.

In my middle-class existence, I forget how much I actually have. Then something—a sermon illustration, a stray thought, a book, a headline, an earthquake, a crisis—shakes me out of my stupor. I feel a tinge of conviction and a desire to change, and I hope this time it really and truly sticks. But when Rachel purchased those tires for our van, then milkshakes for the kids on the way back home, something about her generous response changed things for me.

It wasn't obligation or pity that caused her to cover such a large expense without a second thought. It was empathy.

She thought of all the times she'd been in similar situations, and it gave her joy to be able to help me in my moment of need. And a few months later, I witnessed another beautiful picture of what joyful giving looks like.

In every church I've attended since I was a small child, the offering portion of the service has looked pretty much the same. We stand to sing the doxology, there is a short prayer, and then we all sit and listen to music while the ushers pass brass-colored plates down each row and congregants either drop something in or don't. It's quiet, subdued, and over fairly quickly. But on this particular day, I was attending a special service with my daughter at a local church I'd never been to before, and this offering experience was far from quiet, subdued, or quick.

It started with an enthusiastic message from the pastor, who reminded us why we give and what the money supports. Then the music started, and it was not the sedate organ music or soloist I was used to hearing during offering. This was loud and upbeat and got people up on their feet. Then a gentleman carried a large basket to the front of the church and stood there holding it. I was perplexed about why he just stood there until I realized we were all supposed to walk (or bop to the music if you're my daughter) single file around the perimeter of the sanctuary and drop our offering in the basket before returning to our seats. I quickly looked down to rummage through my purse for some coins for Arsema to place in the basket, and when I lifted my head a moment later, I saw something I'd never seen in church before.

One woman was taking bills out of her wallet and handing them to an older woman next to her. Another was calling out to a friend, who passed her a few bills. As I looked around, I noticed this was happening all around me. Whether or not they had anything in their wallets, everyone was getting up to put something in the offering basket, because everyone who had money was sharing it with those who didn't. This went well beyond giving what little (or much) you could to the church. This was making sure everyone could be part of giving, even if they didn't have anything to give that day. It was beautiful.

When I first realized what was happening, I felt nervous and self-conscious. Aside from the loose change I'd scrounged up from the bottom of my purse for Arsema, I didn't have any cash on me. Nor had I brought a checkbook. It wouldn't have mattered if an offering plate had been quietly and discreetly passed through the pews, but this was not that kind of offering. *They shouldn't do it this way*, I thought. *This makes people feel like they have to give because it's incredibly obvious if they don't.* But that was before I lifted my head from searching my purse and saw all the money changing hands. Then I understood. This offering was a joyous thing to behold. The music was lively, the people were smiling, and no one was left out. There was no embarrassment, no pressure, and no pride, just the joy of giving as a community.

It's easy for me to feel small and overwhelmed when I think about trying to respond to the needs of our global and local neighbors, and I know I'm not alone in feeling that way. Most of us aren't able to write big checks and solve big problems. We have bills of our own to pay and problems of our own to work through. We want to help, but what do we have to offer when war in one part of the world displaces thousands of families and leaves children orphaned? How do we help when our world has a refugee crisis, but we don't live there and don't know what to do? How do we respond when communities in our own country lack safe drinking water and the cost to replace the pipes seems astronomical? What do we do when the department of social services in our own town is overwhelmed and has more children who need safe homes than there are foster parents to care for them? In the face of such enormous and relentless need, what resources could we possibly offer that would make any sort of difference?

Whenever I get that small and overwhelmed feeling, I remember a conversation I had with my mom and my grammy in my late teens. We were standing in the kitchen talking about church, and the topic of giving and tithing came up. Grammy said something I've never forgotten: "Lauren, there are times in life when you don't have a dime to spare. But you can always give of your time and your talent." Generosity doesn't always have to be financial.

A while back, I asked my community of Facebook friends and followers for feedback from single parents. I recognized that I had a blind spot in my life and wanted to know what was hard for them and what they wish parents with partners understood. How could we be better friends and families and churches to the single parents around us? Here are just a few of the responses I received:

- "There is no 'off' button when I have my kiddo. There is no one to ask for help when I'm 'on.' People often say they are jealous when I have a night or weekend off [because my ex-husband has our son]. I can understand, but I feel like they underestimate how they get so many moments off through the week, but I don't have that. I don't have someone to call if I'm running late to grab my son. I have to either pay someone to care for him or turn down work. I don't have family nearby, so making any social plans requires a sitter or bringing my kiddo along. It's also hard not being able to bounce ideas off of someone as I brainstorm how to handle a parenting situation in the moment."—Sara

- "You are in it alone. You have no one to come home to at the end of the day, and build each other up, or brainstorm ideas on how to deal with something, or share funny stories or laughs. It's hard when other moms have their hubby or significant other out of town for a few days and say things like, 'single mom for the week.' If you still have emotional, spiritual, and financial support, you are not a single mom for the week."—Mikel

- "For me, [the hardest thing] is the loneliness, when [the kids] have gone to bed and I sit there on the couch knowing it's just me and me alone."—Samantha

- "The hardest thing [about] single parenting is doing everything all by myself with no help. I wish others understood how hard it is to help my child regulate. So many appointments, not too much time for myself. People could be more welcoming and helpful if they truly understood the spectrum of autism."—Hazel

Hazel's words struck especially close to home. As the mother of two young children with special needs, I tried to imagine what it might have been like to walk my parenting journey alone. I thought about the day Mareto was diagnosed with autism and all the times I sat in waiting rooms while Arsema underwent surgeries. I thought through the therapy appointments and meltdowns and setbacks and even all the successes: the moment Arsema took her first steps, when Mareto started learning to speak, or when the surgeon walked out with the news that everything went fine. What would it have been like to experience all of that alone?

Another mom commented that she never wanted pity because she was a single parent—she was simply raising her children and making sacrifices as any loving parent would. Her words caused me to think more deeply about my emotional response to all the feedback from single parents. Did I feel sad and convicted because I pitied them, or because I regretted unintentionally overlooking them? Sadly, it was a mixture of both. But empathy for another human being isn't supposed to lead us to pity; it's supposed to lead us to action—to extending a helping hand whenever possible and to offering loving support at all times—to being generous with all our resources (time, compassion, and grace included).

So what might it look like to do this? A comment from a single mother named Kneece helped me start to understand better:

> The hardest things are the time restraints and not having another adult to help. For example, my therapy appointment ends at 5:00 in Roseville (30 minutes away with no traffic), but my daughter's basketball practice starts at 5:00. I love when other moms let me tag team with them. Tonight, my friend and neighbor brought both of our daughters to their tutoring center while I was at my Spanish class. Then, I scooped both girls up from tutoring when my class was done. I wish things like this were more commonplace. Can we work together more and help each other out? I feel like I am asking for help a lot because I don't have any other options. I would like my neighbors and friends to let me help them back, more like a parenting neighborhood co-op.

When I read Kneece's comment, I couldn't help but think of that Sunday morning offering when all the little old ladies waved dollar bills at one another with smiles spread across their faces. The joy of generosity is equal opportunity. It happens in giving to one another freely—our help, our time, our possessions—in a back-and-forth manner. The joy of giving is living in community in a way that says, *I got you, and I know you've got me.* Or, as Jesus quite bluntly put it,

"You're far happier giving than getting" (Acts 20:35 THE MESSAGE).

Let's resolve to live wildly generous lives, not because we're the "haves" and others are the "have nots," but because we're all some mix of both.

# THE BUDDY BENCH

Sometimes the people who most need to reach out are
the people least capable of it.
ADELLE DEWITT, *DOLLHOUSE*

Several years ago, the elementary school my children now
attend was intentionally demolished and then rebuilt
on the same lot. I never saw the original structure, but
my son was in kindergarten when the ribbon was cut on
the new building. We toured the halls, marveling at the
bright new rooms and gleaming facilities. His classroom
windows overlooked a roots and shoots garden, a babbling
creek, and a walking trail. The gym even boasted a rock-
climbing wall.

The only downside to starting the year in a new school
was that, while the building was complete and ready for students, the playground was not. The old wooden equipment

still stood in the lot behind the school, but it was taped off—a hazard to the kids. The boards creaked and threatened to collapse, wood was rotting in places, and the slides looked anything but safe. Instead of spending recess on the rickety monkey bars and swings, the kids were ushered to a field on the other side of the school where they could play tag and run off steam.

The following year, just in time for my daughter to enter school, the new playground was finally finished. It is bigger than the first, with more swings and slides and things to climb on. It is handicap accessible, with special swings and seats in the spinning disc for children with mobility issues. I counted all the different places on the playground that allowed for spinning and there are at least five—a tire swing, a stand-up spinner, a bucket spinner, a spinning disc, and a spinning ball. This playground is a delight for children with sensory processing disorders. Even the large xylophone that stands at the perimeter has the pleasant sound of wind chimes on a spring day no matter how hard it is pounded. The designers truly thought of everything.

When the weather is nice, a bunch of other moms and I sit on the benches after school while our kids play and run for an hour or two before we head home to start dinner. I'd sat on those benches a dozen times before I noticed that one of them was branded "Buddy Bench." I looked around at the other benches, but this was the only one with a label.

Later that evening, I asked my kids why one bench on the playground was called the Buddy Bench. My daughter explained, "That's where you sit when you're lonely and don't have anyone to play with."

I was starting to understand. "Then what happens?" I asked.

"Well," she continued, "then someone sees you there and invites you to come play with them."

What a remarkable thing to begin teaching children early in their lives—to be on the lookout for those who need a friend and invite them to join you on your adventures. The Buddy Bench is cultivating empathy in my children and their classmates as they consider what it feels like to need the bench themselves some days and to pay attention to who's sitting there at other times. The result, I hope, will be a group of kids for whom it's second nature to reach out and invite others in.

Sometimes recess can be a difficult time for my son. He doesn't enjoy sports or many of the games other kids his age like to play, so it's not uncommon for him to feel left out. One day he came home from school especially upset, and as I tried to calm him down and figure out the problem, it became clear that, once again, he felt left out at recess. When I asked if he tried sitting on the Buddy Bench, he responded, "I don't do that anymore. I tried and no one came." My heart broke a little, and then I wondered, *Who in my own life doesn't try anymore because no one came?* A Buddy Bench is a nice idea, but it's worthless if no one ever comes when you sit there.

After I asked my Facebook readers who are single parents to share their experiences with me, I scanned my phone and realized I had exactly one single parent in my contacts. Just one. At first I was surprised, but when I took a closer look at my life, it wasn't hard to see why I didn't have many single-parent friends.

I used to participate in a church Bible study for women that met on Tuesday mornings and offered child care. We didn't have any single moms in the group because they had to be at work on Tuesday mornings. The church did offer an evening Bible study for women, but there wasn't any child care available. It also met later in the evening to allow participants time for dinner first. Single mothers who wanted to participate would need to either pay a sitter to watch their kids and handle the bedtime routine, or pay a sitter to watch their kids and keep them up late on a school night so that Mom could do the baths, pj's, stories, and bedtime kisses after she got home. So single mothers weren't really interacting with many of the married women at church in this way.

My own small group of girlfriends consists of married mothers of youngish children. We have a monthly coffee date at someone's house during the week while our kids are at school, and every so often we get together at a local restaurant for a "girls' night out." Each of these gatherings would require a single mom to pay a sitter or miss work in order to join us.

Then there are the moms I hang out with on the playground after school. We chat and laugh and watch our kids play, but again, many single moms are working and don't have the option to join our conversations and build those relationships. So my contact list remains full of mothers who are married, because there is a luxury in my lifestyle I hadn't ever recognized before.

Even the social gatherings that happen on weekends and involve children don't include single parents. The Halloween dinner, the Super Bowl parties, the Easter brunch, the July Fourth cookout—they all include families with two parents and their child(ren). I haven't ever intentionally excluded single parents from my life, but I also haven't ever intentionally included single parents in my life either.

I felt a mixture of sadness and conviction when I considered all the people I hadn't noticed, and I wondered how many of them had waited on a Buddy Bench before giving up.

Sometimes I think we get so caught up in focusing on the people in our immediate orbit that we don't pause to consider who isn't there but maybe should be. When we plan our events, attend Bible studies, set coffee dates and play dates, and go about our daily lives, do we notice who isn't there? Who isn't signing up for summer camp and weekend retreats? Who stopped showing up at the pool or the playground, or never did to begin with? Adult life doesn't provide buddy benches—it's up to us to pay attention to who is missing from our circles. Or, better yet, maybe we could stop circling up all together.

Bestselling author, activist, and internet friend Glennon Doyle encourages her readers to resist the urge to circle up. "If you are standing with other women in a circle and there is a woman standing alone in your circle's vicinity, the thing to do is notice her, smile at her, move over a bit and say, 'Hi, come join us!' Even if she looks at you like you're crazy, inviting her is STILL THE THING TO DO. . . . Also: Horseshoes are better than circles. Leave space. Always leave space."[1]

It may seem uncomfortable, unnatural, and awkward to step out of comfort zones and challenge the status quo, but maybe that's because we Christians have forgotten that's what we're made to do. We weren't created to live up to society's standards and remain comfortably in our bubbles (or circles); we were made to be misfits and rebels and to embrace the unexpected. If we claim to follow Jesus, there is no other way to live.

Jesus is the one who tells us to throw a dinner party but not invite our friends. Instead, he says, "When you give a feast, invite the poor, the crippled, the lame, the blind, and you will be blessed, because they cannot repay you" (Luke 14:13–14).

Now, I'm not in the habit of throwing feasts for my friends, but I am guilty of standing in a circle instead of a horseshoe. If we were to apply Christ's words to our modern-day situation, we might be compelled to reach out to people of a different economic class, faith background, or family structure. Maybe we could have dinner, plan play dates, or hang out at the pool with people who don't normally spend time in our social circles. However we choose to do it, Jesus wants us to break the patterns of exclusion and consider who might be missing. And he places the responsibility for reaching out on us.

Years ago, I remember an older woman at church answering the question of how we could be better at reaching out to young women who feel left out of church events. In a slightly sing-songy voice she said, "I always say, if you want to have a friend you need to be a friend!" Her point being, the responsibility of reaching out was on those who felt left out. I winced at her words. She didn't realize it, but at the time I considered myself one of those young women who felt left out. I was struggling to connect, had grown weary of waiting on the outskirts, and had just about given up. Maybe it's natural to assume that people who want to find friends will actively reach out to others, but for some of us, and during certain seasons of life, that can feel impossibly hard.

We need to recognize that not everyone can find the buddy bench, let alone muster up the effort required to sit on it. It's up to us, all of us, to look out and reach out to one another. It's up to us to always leave room in our lives for one more person. It's up to us to pay attention to who *isn't* there.

Who isn't represented in our churches?
Who comes on Sunday mornings but never attends the
    picnics or dinners?
Who is absent from the field trips and school recitals?
Who avoids book club?
Who doesn't show up at the BBQ or service project or
    conferences and retreats?

Have we made room for others? Have we extended an invitation and then welcomed them with open arms and no strings attached? Or do we huddle up with the same people day after day and tell ourselves that if anyone wants or needs anything from us, they'll ask? The buddy bench is over there, we reassure ourselves, and they can find it if they want to be included. We put the duty of reaching out on others instead of taking responsibility for our neighbors, particularly those we don't immediately see.

✳

When things fall apart, I tend to retreat. I withdraw from life until I can sort out whatever is currently unsorted. I do this partly out of overwhelming fatigue. It takes so much of my mental, emotional, and physical energy just to keep my head above water that I scale back on my typical schedule out of pure necessity and self-care.

A couple of years ago, when we were in the midst of a family crisis, I just about disappeared from every aspect of life outside my home. I might have made an occasional appearance at the playground, but for the most part, I picked the kids up from school and ran back to the car where no one would see my puffy red eyes and exhausted expression. A trip to the grocery store required monumental effort, and the only phone calls I made were to my mom, my husband, and my best friend. Weeks ticked by with each Sunday morning being spent in pajamas, cleaning up the breakfast dishes, and preparing for the week ahead.

After about six weeks of being absent from the church we usually attended, I received a voice mail from the pastor. It was simple and short—just checking in and mentioning that the kids and I were missed. A week or two later, his wife sent a sweet text checking in. It meant the world to me, because no one knew what we were going through. Someone had simply noticed the small thing of our absence. The pastor and his wife had looked around week after week and noted that I wasn't there. Instead of shrugging their shoulders and plowing forward, they paused long enough to reach out when I couldn't.

More recently, on a random Tuesday afternoon, my phone dinged, and I looked down to find a text from my friend Laura: "I miss you! Where are you? I'm not seeing you a single bit!" The pressure of a looming writing deadline was mounting, and I'd all but locked myself in my room with my laptop. I call it my writing cave, and I'd been living there for weeks. When I told her this, she responded with offers to help with the kids when and if needed.

The thing is, I would never have reached out to ask for help. It isn't pride that holds me back; sometimes it just doesn't occur to me. Other times, I don't know what I need. And then there are times when life is too hard and too heavy, and I simply can't lift myself up to the buddy bench.

It isn't enough to proclaim trite phrases such as, "If you want a friend you have to be a friend." It isn't enough to set up a Buddy Bench as a physical reminder that if you want help you must first help yourself. We can't say, "Find the bench and wait there, then we'll come invite you in." No. It isn't enough. We have to start looking out for one another.

The Buddy Bench at my kids' elementary school is a sweet and useful tool in teaching the kids to include others.

But it's just that: a tool, much like training wheels on a bike. The goal of training wheels is to one day not need them anymore. I hope the day will come when they—and we—will reach out to others without having to be asked.

# THIRTEEN

# FOUR HUNDRED AND NINETY TIMES MORE

He who is devoid of the power to forgive is devoid of the
power to love.
MARTIN LUTHER KING JR.

One of the most necessary and inevitable acts of love that empathy naturally leads us into is that of repentance. And repentance is truly an act of love. It is the recognition of how our words, or lack thereof, and our actions, or lack thereof, have impacted our neighbors. It is the experience of true remorse for that impact and the decision to no longer behave in a way that brings pain to those around us. We cannot claim to love our neighbors while ignoring the ways in which we hurt them.

When we step back, look at how our words or actions

impact another person and then think about the situation from their perspective, we are moved to seek forgiveness and walk in a new way. Repentance is more than saying, "I'm sorry." Repentance requires empathy, because we cannot stop our harmful behavior and live differently without it. Without empathy, we'll slip right back into old habits, never understanding what caused the pain in the first place.

Incomplete repentance without empathy looks like saying, "I'm sorry you're hurt." True repentance fueled by empathy says, "I realize now that when I did this it caused you pain. Please forgive me. I won't do that anymore." Repentance screams humility and empathy. It requires a posture totally contrary to pride and defensiveness. It's a lesson I've had to learn the hard way.

When I was a new mom, I was utterly consumed by what was happening in my corner of the world. Those early months weren't easy, but they aren't easy for most moms. I disappeared from view for an extended period of time, totally absorbed with my baby, myself, and our day-to-day life. I was also suffering from a strong case of reverse culture shock in which I was comparing the United States to Ethiopia and harshly judging American materialism and anyone I felt was gripped by it. When I heard complaints about trivial things such as traffic or gassy babies, I would roll my eyes and inwardly chastise the complainers: *That's not a problem. You know what a problem is? Living without clean water and dying of preventable diseases such as malaria and polio.*

One day a friend mentioned a difficult situation to John, and he caught my judgy and exasperated expression in the background. He kindly and gently reminded me, "Hard is hard. We can't judge one person's struggles by what another is going through." I wasn't ready to hear that then, but now I often think of his words and allow them to push me back to empathy.

It was during this season of withdrawal that a dear friend tried to reach out to me. When she called, I took days or even weeks to respond, and when I did, I often couldn't get together or talk for long. She was patient for a time, but one day I opened my email to find a lengthy and somewhat angry message from her. As I read her words, I was struck by a sense of unfairness and a hefty dose of righteous indignation.

*She has a toddler. Doesn't she remember what these baby months are like?*

*My child is sick, and my husband is working full-time and going to school full-time. Can't she give me the grace and space to just get through without the pressure of calling her back?*

*I'm doing the best I can, and if she were a real friend, she would get that!*

I raged inwardly and then sat down to type my response. I was overly polite and passive aggressive in my reply. I refused to apologize, convinced that it was she who should be apologizing to me. We went back and forth on email for a few weeks until we reached the end of the line—she was done, she told me. I'd said things that were unforgivable, and our friendship was over. She wanted me to stop contacting her.

I was surprised that fifteen years of friendship were over in a blink, but even that filled me with a bit of smugness. I read the email aloud to John and asked, "How can she say that? You can't claim to be a Christian and then say someone is unforgivable!" *See?* I assured myself. *She's wrong, and I'm right.* I closed my laptop and went on with life. Never once did I consider that my lack of repentance was equally, if not more, lacking in spiritual fruit.

I grew up in a military family, which meant we moved around a lot and losing friends wasn't foreign to me. But I had always been the one to leave, which meant I'd never had a friend leave me before. It wasn't as easy to move on when everything in life stayed the same except for the absence of this person. I thought about her often, and as time passed, it was with a sense of deep loss and heavy sadness.

Later, through Facebook, I learned she was pregnant, and our back-and-forth messaging had caused her an unhealthy amount of stress in her early pregnancy. With a sting of regret, I wished I had known that. In the following months, I began to unfollow most of our mutual friends on social media—the ones who had really been her friends and not so much mine all along. Seeing their pictures and status updates hurt too much. I missed my friend, though I wouldn't let myself admit it.

Life moved on, and I softened. Over time I regained perspective and no longer judged everyone and everything in my life through the lens of my experiences in Ethiopia. Our family grew, and so did my sense of empathy. The gaping wound of my broken friendship scabbed over in the shape of a jagged scar that was never far from view. Every time something reminded me of my friend, I wished I'd done things differently.

It took time, but eventually I could see things through the eyes of my friend. She had felt rejected by my sudden disappearance from her life. Her initial email had been written out of hurt, not malice. At the time I wasn't able to see it that way, so I felt attacked and misunderstood. Because I hadn't let her in, she'd had trouble seeing life from my perspective too. She didn't understand that my slow response time wasn't a lack of care, but that I was barely treading water. Instead of seeing that I needed help, and maybe some time and space, she thought I was being a careless and aloof friend. If we'd both had more empathy, things could have turned out so differently.

Nearly five years later, I opened Facebook to find a message from my lost friend. It was short but kind, and it left me weeping at my kitchen table. "I think about you a lot," she said, "and, if I'm being honest, I cry when I do." I responded as quickly as I could type and asked if we could talk. We set up a phone call for the following day, and both burst into tears when we got on the phone.

Our friendship is different today. We're different people, we live miles and hours apart, and the words we spoke, the years we spent in silence, and the wounds we inflicted on each other have changed us. But we genuinely love each other. Because of her, I understand acutely the importance of empathy, the necessity of repentance, and the power of forgiveness.

Repentance, I am convinced, is one of the most uncomfortable byproducts of empathy. Empathy seems to come a lot easier when we wrap our arms around someone whose pain has been caused by outside forces. We find it much more difficult to sit with someone bleeding out from wounds we have administered. Avoidance is much easier than repentance, but as we have seen, the easy way is rarely the loving way.

Jemar Tisby begins his book, *The Color of Compromise*, with the story of the bombing of Sixteenth Street Baptist Church in Birmingham, Alabama, in September 1963. Four young girls, just out of Sunday school and readying themselves for the soon-to-begin Youth Day service, were killed in the blast. Tisby tells of a speech given by a young, white lawyer named Charles Morgan Jr. the day after the bombing, where he asks an all-white young men's club, "Who did it? Who threw that bomb? Was it a Negro or a white? The answer should be, 'We all did it.' Every last one of us is condemned for that crime and the bombing before it and a decade ago. We all did it."[1] As a result, Morgan received numerous death threats so serious that he eventually closed his law practice and moved his family out of the area.

The call to repentance isn't easy, but it is necessary. As Tisby wrote, "History and Scripture teach us that there can be no reconciliation without repentance. There can be no repentance without confession. And there can be no confession without truth."[2] If we want to love our neighbors, we have to tell the truth—first to ourselves, then to God, then to others.

Over ten years ago I was at a church gathering with dozens of other young adults. An older man, an elder, was giving a message to the group designed to encourage them to continue to walk with God well after they had moved on to other seasons of life. He wanted to be encouraging and funny, so he pointed to my husband and told the story of John turning back to faith in his senior year of college. As it turns out, that time also coincided with the beginning of our dating relationship, which this man made clear. With zero effort at subtlety, he exclaimed, "Guys! Look what can happen when you walk with God!" as he pointed enthusiastically at me. I felt my cheeks grow warm as I realized what was happening. I was the prop in this story, the trophy for a man who had made a good choice.

He continued to wave his hand in my direction as laughter erupted among the young men in attendance. "Look at her! Look!" I chuckled nervously, wanting the ground to swallow me whole. Half joking, he proclaimed to them all, "If you follow God, look what he'll give you!"

I locked eyes with John, who was also turning a bit red. The laughter continued until I heard the man's wife mercifully call out, "That's enough!" The laughter died down and the message continued, followed by a picnic.

It wasn't the first time, and certainly wouldn't be the last time, I was treated like an object rather than a person. But it was perhaps the only time it was so explicitly declared to a large group of young men who were invited to survey me while I sat there, swallowing shame that didn't belong to me. I knew it wasn't right, but I had been conditioned to believe these things weren't really a big deal, so I shook it off and bit into my fried chicken, determined to enjoy the rest of the afternoon.

Just as John and I were preparing to leave the event, the man who had given the message approached us. "Lauren, I need to apologize to you for what I said."

I was immediately uncomfortable, so I laughed it off. "Oh, that's okay!" I said with a dismissive wave of my hand.

"No. It isn't," he insisted. "Please let me ask for forgiveness."

He went on to confess exactly what he had done wrong. That he made me the object of a cheap laugh as he enjoyed an entertained audience. That he had objectified me for points among the guys. That his wife had later pointed out what he had done and that he realized it was hurtful. Then he apologized and asked, "Will you please forgive me?"

I swallowed. "Yes," I replied. And I meant it then as much as I have the dozens of times I've chosen to forgive him all over again since that day. Like the time an older man followed me from the grocery store checkout line all the way to my car to compliment my body and appearance and it brought back the memory of that afternoon by the river. Like when politicians and public figures excuse jokes about sexual assault as "locker room talk," and I can hear those eighteen-to-twenty-two-year-olds laughing. Like the time I was catcalled as I walked up the sidewalk with my two young children and heard "Look at her!" and saw the finger pointing in my direction; I felt the pain and embarrassment of that day all over again.

I wonder sometimes if this is why Jesus told us we need to forgive each other 490 times or seventy times more than the seven times his disciples thought they were required to (Matthew 18:22). Of course, what he's really saying is that there should be no limit on our willingness to forgive, because there will be no limit to the times repentance and forgiveness will be necessary to continue relationships and be a neighbor to one another. The truth is, we need to forgive 490 times more than we might want to, yes, and we also need to repent at least that much.

❧

Sometimes we get confused about what this cycle of repentance and forgiveness is supposed to look like. We think that our presence is required for healing to occur, but I am learning that sometimes the opposite is true and the first step toward forgiveness is walking away. Distance has a way of clearing our vision. What was once blurred by anger, hurt, pride, and defensiveness can be brought into sharper focus with the benefit of time and space, allowing us to see one another with a little more understanding. I have recently been struck by how distance can spur repentance over the treatment of those in the LGBTQ+ community.

*Queer Eye for the Straight Guy* began airing when I was in college and was mostly watching reruns of *Law and Order* with my freshman roommate. The only reality television we indulged in at that time was the first season of *American Idol*, when we piled into our friend's dorm room once a week to watch Simon, Paula, and Randy judge a group of hopeful singers. We were far more focused on whether Kelly and Justin were actually a couple than the makeovers that were happening on Bravo. So when *Queer Eye* came back in a new iteration via Netflix, it was barely a blip on my radar. I finally decided to give the show a try after I kept seeing people I respected online describe it using words like "life-changing," "mind-blowing," and a "must-watch."

I rarely binge-watch shows, but once I started watching *Queer Eye*, I couldn't stop. John teased me a little at first. "Are you crying *again*?" he'd laugh. But eventually he watched a few episodes with me. I love Tan's style and kindness. JVN's zest and sass make me literally laugh out loud. Antoni makes me crave guacamole and smile at his boyish antics. Karamo makes me stand a little taller and nod along with his wisdom and pep talk. But Bobby makes me cry and see a world I always thought I knew in a different way.

When Bobby talks about growing up in an extremely religious home as a gay child, I grieve. When he describes, through tears, begging God to change him—to make him like girls—I weep with him. And when he tells the story of leaving the church and leaving his home at fifteen, I understand. He had been told he was an abomination from the people he loved most his whole life, before he even knew how to spell a word like *abomination*. The final straw came when he was outed to his family and his own mother looked him in the eye and said, "I know. And it disgusts me." So Bobby left.

His story is, sadly, not uncommon. Throughout the series, we are introduced to young people who have been shunned by their loved ones, their churches, and their communities for being gay. My heart shattered a thousand times as I listened to their stories, the stories I never get to hear from the pulpit or the prayer groups or the Bible studies. Sometimes they've been kicked out, told they aren't welcome, and other times they've chosen to leave and not subject themselves to any more abuse, discrimination, degradation, and harm. In some cases the exodus has been the very thing that brought about repentance.

One particularly poignant episode of *Queer Eye* features a woman we come to know as Mama Tammye. Mama Tammye is a deeply loving, warm, joyful woman who is also deeply religious. She is an integral part of her church community, and you can quickly tell that her church is her family. Then we learn that Mama Tammye's son, Miles, is gay and that he left the church a while ago. She wants him to come to a special homecoming service, but he isn't too sure.

Miles walked away from a community he loved and an important part of himself—singing in the church choir—because it was too hard to be a gay boy in church. But this distance caused repentance in his own mother's heart. She began to see things through his eyes, to see the church experience from his perspective, and she began to understand. His absence led her to empathy, and empathy led her to repentance. In an interview, Mama Tammye described the moment she realized she was wrong:

> Jesus spoke to me and said, "You say you have the same heart and mind that I do, so why can't you see your son the way I do? Why can't you love him the way I do?" I never told Miles anything like "get out of my house," but I thought I was building him up with love when I was really doing the opposite. I asked him for forgiveness.[3]

By the end of the episode, we see Miles walk hand in hand with his mother into the church he left.

Not every story ends like this, but some do. Sometimes

walking away is the catalyst for repentance and forgiveness. Sometimes the absence of people we love leads us to ask ourselves why they left, and sometimes we'll find that the answer is us. When my friend chose to end the ongoing email conversation and, by extension, our friendship, the space between us drove me to consider her point of view. The pangs of missing her presence in my life caused me to pause and look again at my own words and actions and how they had impacted her. Absence led me to empathy, and empathy led me to repentance, and repentance led me to forgiveness. I hope that the flight of LGBTQ+ brothers and sisters from our pews leads to the same in the church. May we feel their absence, be driven to empathy, examine our role in their pain, and kneel in repentance.

According to *USA Today*, one of Martin Luther King Jr.'s most tweeted quotes is, "Forgiveness is not an occasional act; it is a constant attitude."[4] This from a man who was rarely on the receiving end of the empathy he and so many others needed and deserved. It highlights to me, in modern language, what Jesus was trying to convey when he answered the question about how we ought to forgive others. Forgiveness isn't a one-time thing; it's a lifestyle. If someone is forgiving, that typically means another is repenting, and we will find ourselves at both ends of that seesaw more often than we find comfortable. The back and forth of forgiveness and repentance is the only way to survive and thrive in community with others.

Life gives us all sorts of pressure and stress and challenges. On our best days, we handle them well, but on average or worse days, we fall short. All of us are still in the process of becoming the best version of ourselves, which means we all need grace. Instead of rushing to judgment or defensiveness when our mess collides with another's, we can slow down, inhale a large dose of empathy, and, depending on our role in any given moment of pain, repent or forgive 490 times more.

# THE INTERNET IS STILL REAL LIFE

The internet is becoming the town square for the global
village of tomorrow.

BILL GATES

I met my friend Wynne via the internet. This was back in
the golden age of blogging, when most of us were still on
blogspot.com and posted almost daily with content as simple
as a recipe, a random train of thought, or a family trip to the
strawberry farm. Our blogs had cliché titles such as "Living
by Faith" and "Love Makes a Family." We found other blog-
gers writing about similar topics and left comments on their
posts, which usually resulted in a comment back. This is
how Wynne and I found each other, even though she lives in
Texas and I reside in Virginia.

A couple of years later, we realized we were both attending the same conference and neither of us had a roommate, so we decided to room together at the hotel. I met her in person for the first time at the airport baggage claim, and when I rounded the corner to find her waiting, we both squealed and hugged like we'd been buddies since grade school. Wynne and I chatted nonstop for the hour-long drive from the airport to the conference center and stayed up into the early morning hours talking about everything from books and clothes to infertility and grief. When the weekend ended, we continued to stay in touch online.

A little over a year later, John and I flew to Ethiopia to meet our daughter, and Wynne happened to be living in the capital city of Addis Ababa, where we were staying for the week. A professional photographer, she brought her equipment and met us at our hotel the morning we first went to see Arsema. She was there, quietly snapping photos in the background, when we first held our baby girl. She captured one of the most pivotal moments of our lives so that we could have those memories in picture form forever. And we have this all because one day she left a comment on one of my blog posts.

It's true that the internet can be a distraction from the people in our face-to-face world, pulling us away from relationships we've built through time, shared experiences, and daily life. But it can also expand our horizons, introduce us to people and experiences we might not otherwise know about, and enrich our lives. When we approach our online relationships with the same consideration we extend to our face-to-face relationships, good things can happen.

Conversely, when we forget the humanity of the people on the other side of our screens, we can do more damage than we might ever realize.

❧

When one of my blog posts first went viral, it was a dizzying experience. I struggled to keep up with the influx of emails crowding my inbox, the notifications on my Facebook page, and the new followers suddenly appearing on Instagram. I hadn't yet figured out Twitter, which is probably a good thing. The attention was fun and exciting at first. I had sweet and moving messages to read, publications asking me to write for them, and even television producers calling to chat. It all seemed a little strange and silly, but fun if I kept things in perspective and didn't get too caught up in it all. Although the sudden attention made me a little anxious, most people had been kind. Unfortunately, that all changed by the end of the week.

It started with one email that made my blood run cold. I couldn't believe the hateful and vile words that appeared in front of me in black and white. Shocked, I read them a second time, and my hands shook as I clicked the trash icon at the top of the email. I tried to shake the message from my mind but felt queasy about it for the rest of the morning. When I returned to my inbox later in the day, I found dozens more messages similar to the one I'd deleted earlier. Through a blur of tears, I clicked through and deleted each one. The emails made threats against my children, expressed hopes for my death, and were filled with the vilest of slurs and evil words. I sobbed at my kitchen table as I cast them all into the void. I closed my laptop and hoped it was over. It wasn't.

The next day I discovered the comments section on my blog had been overrun by similar messages, and so had my Facebook page. Baffled, I tried to figure out where this vitriol was coming from. It turned out that a few different websites had shared my viral post with their communities, which were filled with people who held pretty hateful views. The group was unknown to me at the time, but now we know them as the "alt-right," a white nationalist movement.

I closed down comments on my blog and never reopened them. I figured out how to filter certain words from coming through in my messages and blocked a number of users from commenting on or viewing my posts. When a few weeks passed with no more hate mail, I breathed a sigh of relief that it was all over. It had been painful and a waste of time, but I had gotten through it. A few months later, a new wave of emails started, and then it happened a few more times until it finally tapered off about a year later. *Good riddance*, I thought.

But it wasn't over. On the morning of November 9, 2016, the day after Election Day, I woke up, made breakfast for the kids, and drove them to school before coming home to pour a large mug of coffee for myself and check the news. After reading a few articles, I logged into Twitter and immediately wished I could crawl back into bed and wake up in an alternate reality.

My notifications number was much higher than usual, which was odd because I hadn't tweeted anything in days, perhaps longer. I nervously clicked the notifications icon and found tweet after tweet attacking my children, my family, and me. Someone had gleefully imposed threats of deportation and racial slurs over stolen photos of my kids. Taunts and threats and hate screamed at me through the screen, and I broke down. I wanted to scream back, *I am a person, and this is my family! We are real and normal and human! Enough!* Instead, I took an Advil and a few screenshots. I was sick of deleting, ignoring, and pretending nothing was happening; I wanted to publicly call out the behavior.

I posted a couple of screenshots to my Facebook friends, letting them know what hate on the internet looks like. Immediately, the post was filled with words of shock, sympathy, concern, and even outrage. Most people were horrified that I'd dealt with this off and on for a couple of years, and all condemned the behavior. But what was so interesting to me was that a few of the people who commented to express their disgust had previously engaged in similar behavior. I'd seen them viciously attack public figures who held different views than they did. I'd seen them dehumanize politicians who challenged their world views or practiced a different faith. I'd seen them literally damn groups of people to hell for things they didn't agree with. And yet, here they were in my comment section saying it was clearly wrong for these strangers to be so cruel to me and my family. Why the disconnect? I can't know for certain, but I have a feeling the difference between me and all those people they attacked regularly, in their minds, was that they knew me and my family in person. Those other people were just on the internet, and sometimes we allow a screen to rob us of our empathy and basic human kindness.

What is it about a computer screen and an avatar that strips us of our ability to remember that a flesh-and-blood person is represented by each screen name? Provided that we aren't all following a bunch of bots, when we engage in an online conversation, we are talking to actual people— people with lives and families and jobs and churches and friends. But something about typed letters in black with a bright white background makes us forget that there are still stories behind those words and feelings behind each profile picture.

Suppose you and I have a difference of opinion about a theological issue. Suppose this issue concerns how to best extend love to our neighbors who belong to other faith groups. You see things one way, and I see them another. If you were to walk up to me in a grocery store parking lot and say, "You obviously don't care about Jesus or the gospel. You are an instrument of the devil, and you are going to burn in hell," you would see my face register shock before crumpling into a hurt expression. You might see the color drain from my cheeks or my hands begin to shake. You might even see me cry. Seeing my reaction would likely elicit some sort of response in you because you aren't a robot carved from a block of ice. You might not show it, but you'd feel a tinge of discomfort because you'd be confronted with the impact of your words. You might even think about it later, and being forced to consider my feelings, perhaps you'd choose your words with greater care in the future.

Now suppose this same exchange happens online instead

of in person. Suppose we comment back and forth about our difference of opinions, and then you decide to post the same parking lot accusation as a status update for me and the rest of the world to view. You click "publish" and walk away from the computer. You don't ever see the impact of your words. You don't see my response—the shock and hurt, the tears and the sadness. Because you never have to see the consequence of your actions, you aren't triggered by conscience or empathy in the way you would be if you'd said those things to my face.

A couple thousand years ago, Jesus went to the top of a mountain and sat down. He looked out at the throngs of people sitting all around him and began to speak. Today, we refer to his message as the Sermon on the Mount, and it is perhaps the most beautiful, poetic, hopeful, and convicting sermon the world has ever heard. It begins with a series of blessings called the Beatitudes.

> Blessed are the poor in spirit, for theirs is the kingdom of heaven.
> Blessed are those who mourn, for they shall be comforted.
> Blessed are the meek, for they shall inherit the earth.
> Blessed are those who hunger and thirst for righteousness, for they shall be satisfied.
> Blessed are the merciful, for they shall receive mercy.
> Blessed are the pure in heart, for they shall see God.

Blessed are the peacemakers, for they shall be called
    sons of God.
Blessed are those who are persecuted for righteousness'
    sake, for theirs is the kingdom of heaven.
Blessed are you when others revile you and persecute
    you and utter all kinds of evil against you falsely on
    my account. Rejoice and be glad, for your reward is
    great in heaven, for so they persecuted the prophets
    who were before you. (Matthew 5:3–12)

What I see in this list is not only hope for anyone who identifies with one of the blesseds Christ described, but a prescription for life. As one might say online, #goals. This is who we are to be and how we are to treat others: with meekness and mercy and a heart for peace. Nowhere in the Bible does Jesus excuse or tolerate cruelty, threats, arrogance, and pride. I read these words and feel convicted of all the times I've typed angry and arrogant words into cyberspace.

Who we are and how we behave online matters. It matters because all of life—from the playground, to the boardroom, the gym, and the Twitter feed—is real life. When we remember that, we can reclaim the internet as a place where empathy thrives. And if you don't believe that's possible, I've got just the story for you.

The beginning of the story is sadly quite ordinary for social media—a sixty-four-year-old man named Michael Beatty came across a tweet in which actor and comedian Patton Oswalt expressed political views Beatty disagreed with. Beatty was in a bad mood and fired off a few quick tweets insulting Oswalt's acting, as well as his physical appearance. Initially Oswalt responded in kind, but then he went to Beatty's profile and discovered that he'd been experiencing some serious medical struggles and wasn't able to cover his bills. In a moment of true empathy, Oswalt put himself in Beatty's shoes and realized he'd be pretty cranky too. So he made a decision to respond in love.

Not only did Oswalt donate to the GoFundMe account Beatty had set up to raise the money to pay his medical bills, he also encouraged his 4.5 million Twitter followers to do the same. By the end of the week, the original fundraising goal of $5,000 had been exceeded by $26,000. It was a beautiful moment for all involved. Beatty later posted on Twitter,

> "@pattonoswalt managed to not only let me slide on a rough tweet to him, but started something that has me reevaluating friendships and productive dialogue regardless of political affiliation. . . . Patton, you have humbled me to the point where I can barely compose my words. You have caused me to take pause and reflect on how harmful words from my mouth could result in such an outpouring."[1]

I hope exchanges like this one are just the beginning of a new trend online where the internet can be used to build up instead of tear down, to help instead of hurt, to advocate instead of attack, and to spread love instead of hate. This is possible if we remember that behind every screen is a person, every person has a story and feelings, and how we treat them online impacts them in real life.

In spite of plenty of evidence that points to the contrary, I see great potential for the internet's role in helping us love our neighbors well. If we let it, the internet opens the door to worlds that previously remained unseen and unknown to us. Like when we all got a front-row view of the war in Syria when Bana Alabed, just seven years old, tweeted from Aleppo while hiding under her mattress from the falling bombs. In an often-forgotten corner of the world, her story and pictures helped us to pause and remember the suffering of others. To care. To feel with her as she tweeted something as simple as, "I'm reading to forget the war."[2]

While it has its flaws, the internet "gives us plenty of ways to see past our own reflections."[3] We get to choose how we use the internet and how we let it influence us. We get to choose to take the online world as seriously as the "IRL" world and remember the humanity of all its users. We can allow the internet to be a window to the world and an opportunity for us to step into each other's shoes for a little while each time we log on. In doing so, we can create online neighborhoods that reflect the ones outside our front doors—neighborhoods where we care for each other's needs, share recipes, practice compassion and grace and humility, and learn from one another.

## FIFTEEN

# PASS THE MIC

Sometimes all it takes is a voice, one voice that becomes a hundred, then a thousand, unless it's silenced.
BRYAN DENTON, *NEWSIES*

**N**ewsies was one of my favorite movies when I was grow-ing up. Our cousins owned a copy on VHS, and we watched it every time we visited their home in Pennsylvania. I recently watched it with my daughter and was caught up in the rousing anthems and youthful exuberance all over again.

Based on the newsboys' strike of 1899, the musical tells the story of one newsboy, Jack Kelly, who rallies other new-sies to fight for justice when the newspaper publisher raises prices at their expense. The climax of the film, for me, is when the ragtag group—consisting of Jack, siblings Davey, Sarah, and Les, and a reporter named Bryan Denton—break into the basement of publishing giant Joseph Pulitzer and

173

discover old printing presses. The newsboys' strike has been shut out of all the papers and can't gain traction because the general public and other child laborers aren't hearing about it. They use the old presses to print their own paper and distribute copies to every child laborer they find in New York City. Then they wait in front of the newspaper building, and soon the streets are filled with youth marching to support the newsboys' strike. They each raise their voices in chants that thunder up the high-rise building to the ears of Mr. Pulitzer. The strike ends, the newsboys get a fair wage, and everyone goes back to work.

Watching *Newsies* as a child made me feel like I was invincible and there was no end to what I could achieve with the power of my own motivation, some dedicated friends, an awesome soundtrack, and the strength of my own voice. Watching it as an adult, I'm far more aware of how power imbalances and oppressive systems can silence those who are oppressed, which leads me to have a bit of a different reaction to the film. I still feel fired up and ready to take on a cause, but I am also aware that how I use my power, my voice, and my platform matters. While I once imagined myself in the role of one of the child activists, such as Jack Kelly, I now find myself more inspired by the eager yet wise reporter, Bryan Denton.

Throughout the movie it becomes clear that Denton is motivated to help the newsies because he sincerely believes their cause matters. When he sees they are being oppressed, instead of standing up and shouting about it himself, he passes the megaphone (or printing press, as it were) to the boys themselves. Where others might have used the newsies' cause to insert themselves into the center of the story, Denton steps to the side, allowing the boys to take center stage. Then he works to amplify their voices.

When they needed someone to share their words and actions, Denton was there, willing to put his job on the line to print their story.

When they were arrested and didn't have money to post bond, Denton was there, bailing each one out of jail.

When they were hungry, he fed them.

When they got discouraged, he built them up.

When the paper he worked for refused to print stories about the newsboys' strike, he helped them start their own paper.

When all hope seemed lost, Denton brought the newsboys' voices to the ear of the governor, who brought to justice those who had abused their authority.

Every step of the way, Denton used his power, resources, privilege, and time to help one of the most marginalized communities in New York City at the turn of the twentieth century—child laborers. With each success he made sure the boys knew it was their own hard work and passion that brought them victory. He didn't try to be their voice; he amplified the voice they already had.

It was just a few weeks before Mareto's second birthday when a doctor told us our son was on the autism spectrum. At first I was filled with fear of the future and heartbreak for all I imagined was lost. The initial months following the diagnosis were overwhelming as we did our best to navigate a new world suddenly filled with binders of information, visits from homecare service providers, and therapy services. We set up a trampoline in the corner of Mareto's bedroom and a special swing in the middle of the living room. We bought sensory toys and organized them in bins. We filled prescriptions, stayed up late reading the latest research, and were unwavering in our efforts to do everything possible to give our son what he needed to have an amazing life.

Fear and heartbreak shifted to zeal as I determined that I would become a fierce advocate for Mareto. There were times my passion was laser-focused in ways that were beneficial for all, such as my relentless phone calls to staff at the children's hospital. When they told me the waiting list to see a certain specialist was over a year long, I thanked them, hung up, and called back the next morning. I called every morning for six weeks until they gave us an appointment. Even when they asked me to stop calling, even when they assured me they'd taken my name and number and would call if there was a cancellation, I kept calling. When we met similar dismissals from the social services office, I did my research and spent months fighting to get my son the services he needed and was entitled to by law. I finally reached the person who could help, and someone was in our home to provide care within weeks. This advocacy was good and helpful and right. My son couldn't do these things himself, and he needed me to fight with and for him in those ways.

As time passed, Mareto's vocabulary grew, and he began to share his needs with a clarity many adults don't possess. He is incredibly in tune to his feelings and has a unique ability to express them. Usually, if we don't understand what Mareto is trying to tell us, the fault is our lack of listening rather than his lack of speaking up. Now, a shift is occurring in our relationship and his life, and I sometimes struggle to move with it. I have gotten so used to speaking for Mareto, to deciding what he needs and plowing toward it full steam ahead, that it has taken concerted effort (and many missteps) to step back and let him speak for himself. With each new day comes a reminder that to be his advocate now means to amplify his voice rather than speak over it with my own.

Recently I was invited to a screening of a documentary called *Intelligent Lives*. Narrated by actor Chris Cooper, the film follows the lives of three young adults with varying disabilities. Micah, Naieer, and Naomie are in different transitional phases of life—Micah is in college, Naieer is finishing high school and considering going to art school, and Naomie is interning at a beauty school with the hopes of securing a full-time job. The film explores how the general population tends to silence and dismiss people with intellectual disabilities and also highlights how much is lost when that happens.

One of my favorite parts of the film is when Micah signs paperwork to transfer guardianship from his parents to himself. "I call the shots!" he declares with pride. I couldn't help but grin along with him, because this particular situation wasn't the result of breaking away from an abusive relationship but the natural result of growing up in a family that chose to empower him. A separate scene shows his parents reminiscing about IEP meetings, and they note that Micah started attending them when he was in fifth grade. The idea was that Micah should have a voice in meetings that were about him, his future, and his services. Of course, stated like that, it seems incredibly obvious, but disabled individuals are one of the most silenced and ignored groups in society.

The film reminded me of a statement I'd read on the website for the Autistic Self Advocacy Network. Here's how they describe their mission: "to empower autistic people across the world to take control of our own lives and the future of our common community, and seek to organize the autistic community to ensure our voices are heard in the national conversation about us." Their slogan is "Nothing about us without us!"[1] It's a slogan I love, but it also gives me pause.

How many times have I engaged in conversations about issues that aren't about me without considering the perspectives of those who actually are impacted? How many times have I seen public officials make policies without ever engaging the individuals affected by those policies? How many times have I sat in church meetings as someone pontificates about what is needed in a community on the other side of the world, all the while never bothering to ask the people in that community what they need or want? When I initially wrestled with these questions, it was hard not to wonder how I might feel if the tables were turned. And then it hit me—I know exactly how I'd feel.

I was in tenth grade when my high school guidance counselor set up a meeting with my parents to discuss my future. The previous summer, after several tests, it was discovered that I had a learning disability. I was given an

IEP and an hour in the resource room each school day. My grades began to improve, and it was time to make a decision about which direction I would pursue for the rest of my high school career. Our school offered two diplomas: a standard diploma or an advanced diploma. Colleges only accepted applicants with an advanced diploma, and in my mind, it wasn't even a question which one I'd pursue.

We sat down in the counselor's office for our meeting, and she began to go over my options for classes for the next couple of years. As she spoke, I realized she was only covering my choices for a standard diploma. When I pointed this out, it became clear that she didn't consider an advanced diploma an option for me. She'd looked at my file, made a decision about what would be best for me, and conducted the meeting without ever asking me how I felt about it. I felt small, insignificant, and belittled. This person didn't care what I thought or felt about my own future, and my voice wasn't important to her. In her mind, she was being helpful, but to me it felt dismissive and degrading.

I summoned my courage, took a deep breath, and spoke up. Stopping her mid-sentence, I firmly declared, "No. I am getting an advanced diploma, and I am going to college." My parents smiled and stared back at the guidance counselor with a look that said, *She has spoken. What are you going to do about it?* The tone of the meeting shifted, and a plan was put in place for me to achieve the goals and dreams *I* had set for *myself*.

But what if I had been left out of the meeting entirely? What if the adults in the room—the people with more power and authority—had gotten together and made decisions based on what they felt was good and right without considering my point of view? That's an unfortunate dynamic that happens a lot—and not just to people who are disabled. It happens to every community marginalized to the sidelines of power. Which is why we have to ask ourselves some tough questions. What would it look like to turn our power structures upside down and give those on the sidelines an opportunity to be heard? What might we learn, and how might we grow? Who are we harming when we insist on hoarding the narrative—speaking as if ours is the only perspective? When we share only one side of a multifaceted story, we unintentionally create blind spots in ourselves and others. But passing the mic to others, who haven't always been given the opportunity to share, gives us a more complete picture of our figurative neighborhoods and shows us how we can be a better neighbor.

Every community, every culture, every church has a narrative. These narratives are the lens through which we see and make sense of the world. It's how a community makes meaning of the past, interprets the present, and charts a course to the future. The voices that contribute to a narrative have the power to shape collective knowledge, understanding, and calls to action. Conversely, the voices that don't contribute to a narrative are disempowered.

When tales of conquests of land and resources are only told from the colonizers' perspectives, for example, they become the hero of the story, and the voices of those who were oppressed and enslaved and stolen from are excluded from the narrative. We learn an incomplete history, which prevents us from understanding the struggles some nations and communities face today. So instead of understanding, and even repentance, we offer judgment and ridicule.

When the only knowledge we have of police shootings comes from a report the officer fills out, and a poorly chosen photograph of the victim is plastered on the nightly news programs, we form a narrative in our minds about what happened that often leads us to believe the shooting was justified, deserved even. But cell phone footage, and dashboard cameras, and family members sharing about the person they knew and loved tell a different side to the story, and suddenly the narrative shifts.

When men are the only ones allowed to speak from the pulpit and teach in church, we lose the perspective and knowledge and expression of God on earth in half its inhabitants. We create an environment ripe for the abuse of girls and women as they are shut out of positions that hold any sort of power and their voices are consistently sidelined and silenced.

We need to pass the mic every now and then.

It's as simple as reexamining the books on our shelves and the podcasts saved to our phones. Do we include perspectives that differ from our own? Are we following voices of color, LGBTQ+ voices, and disabled voices on social media?

Passing the mic often looks like expanding the catalog of voices we listen to and then sharing them with those around us. Recommend books written by black authors. Share a podcast or an article by an Indigenous writer. Repost content on social media platforms from People of Color and those on the LGBTQ+ spectrum. Watch talks given by disability activists. Listen to women, vote for women, support women.

Sometimes passing the mic takes on a more literal role, and it looks like inviting a new voice to the platform and the pulpit. How much richer would our congregations be if the voices that are typically silenced could step up to the microphone and tell their stories?

What would we learn about the power and love and grace of Jesus through the story of a man struggling with alcoholism?

A single mother working the night shift?

A family going through homelessness?

A person recently released from jail?

The parents of a teenager lost to gun violence?

A refugee or immigrant or migrant worker?

A person who speaks English as a second language or who speaks through sign language?

A family living in poverty?

A child?

I wonder how our view of the gospel and the hope of Jesus Christ might grow with these voices speaking to us. I wonder how our neighbor love might change when we stop speaking for them and allow them to speak for themselves.

In an essay about women's ministry, author Sarah Bessey wrote a line that I think about often: "No more celebrity speakers, please just hand the microphone to that lady over there that brought the apples."[2] When I'm tempted to hog the spotlight, talk for others, or insert myself in a story that doesn't belong to me, I remind myself to *pass the mic to the lady with the apples*. It's my way of telling myself to step aside and amplify someone else's voice—a quirky reminder to be more like my *Newsies* hero, Bryan Denton.

There is no such thing as a voiceless people. Marginalized and oppressed groups are and have been speaking out for ages, but some of us have been hogging the microphone. In doing so, we rob others of their story and the power that comes with sharing it. Sometimes love looks like passing the mic and slipping backstage to make sure the speakers work and the volume is turned up.

# SIXTEEN

# COMFORT VS. CRITICISM

Let me never fall into the vulgar mistake
of dreaming that I am persecuted
whenever I am contradicted.
RALPH WALDO EMERSON

I'm part of a fairly coddled category of people. I'm an American, Christian, middle-class, white, suburban, college-educated, heterosexual, married mother of two. I'm slender, healthy, and don't have a terrible sense of style (though I won't be gracing any *Vogue* covers or picking up a modeling gig anytime soon). When we moved a few years ago and I requested my medical records to take to a new practice, I noticed in browsing through them that one physician had noted I was "well-groomed." I'll take it. I say all this not to boast or boost my image but to explain that I fit the description for people generally considered acceptable or praiseworthy just for being me. I'm not someone who is often singled out for criticism.

I'm also a middle child, which means my life motto has been "fly under the radar." As a kid I was content to let my older sister be my guinea pig. When she tested boundaries (or sailed right past them), I watched carefully to see how my parents reacted and what happened to her. When things blew up, I made a mental note to avoid the behavior she'd engaged in. I was also paying close attention to what garnered her rewards, praise, and success. For better or worse, I was watching, striving to mimic the things that reaped benefits and avoid the things that didn't. It was a strategy that served me well for the most part, and I owe my sister a debt of gratitude for paving the way for me to coast along on middle ground.

So you see how the random collection of advantageous circumstances that have shaped my life have, through no merit of my own, set me up for a pretty comfortable life, if I so choose.

Now that the stage is appropriately set, it should come as no great surprise when I admit that I haven't always handled criticism well. There are probably a handful of reasons for this, personality type being one of them, but the most obvious is that I haven't had a lot of experience receiving criticism. So when it first came my way, it startled me. My initial response was to shut down and bow out. Avoidance. As author Elbert Hubbard once wrote, to avoid criticism, "say nothing, do nothing, be nothing."[1]

A few years ago, a Twitter conversation broke out among a bunch of Christian women I follow. The details are blurry in my memory, but what I do remember is that several women I had admired from afar, and some with whom I had formed an online friendship, joined in a conversation about "platform" (a fancy word for audience/followers) and faith and blogging and book marketing. Some of the comments were fascinating, some were over my head, and some I'd heard many times before. I watched from the sidelines as bigger publications and more "famous" authors started tweeting about it, and then, suddenly, I wanted in.

I started out feeling a little tentative because Twitter makes me nervous. One of my first interactions on Twitter was with bestselling author Jon Acuff. I responded to a question he put out, and my tweet had so many typos that it didn't make sense. It was so bad he responded, "Wow. Autocorrect really got you there." To which I nonsensically replied, "Wools." My phone had autocorrected "Whoops." He tweeted back something about giving up. I was so mortified I deactivated my Twitter account for at least a year. I wish I were joking. When I tweet now, I do so with caution and a bit more backbone. All of which is to say, my first contribution to this massive thread about platform and faith and blogging was short and simple.

To my surprise, I received positive responses from several of the women, some of whom I'd never interacted with before. For the next couple of days, I enjoyed engaging off and on in this conversation. Then, somewhere along the way, I noticed a tweet from a black woman who pointed out how privileged the whole conversation was and that none of it applied to women of color. When she outlined exactly why that was, I felt convicted.

Her perspective was eye-opening for two reasons—first, because I'd never thought of it from her point of view, and second, because I had failed to even consider that there might be another point of view. I reached out and tweeted, "Wow, I never thought of it like that. Thanks for sharing." To which she and two other women of color responded with their own version of, *Yeah, amazing things happen when you listen to women of color!*

Intellectually, I understood that their responses were pointed but also good-natured. These were women who expressed both wisdom and legitimate frustration born from years of being overlooked or dismissed by people just like me. But I admit I also felt scolded, and though it embarrasses me to admit it, here are some of the thoughts that ran through my mind:

- You don't know me at all! I have women of color in my life that I listen to regularly! (Obviously not enough.)
- Ummm. I'm RAISING a woman of color. (Yes, I know—all the more reason to be listening to more of them. I now want to smack my head against the table too.)
- My best friend is a woman of color, so there! (Ahh yes, the black friend we white people love to trot out to prove we're "woke.")
- Are you implying that I'm racist? How dare you? (They weren't, I don't think, but if they had been, they wouldn't have been wrong. Living in a society formed and run by racist people, systems, and structures impacts me in more ways than I readily realize.)

I shut down my computer and chewed on her words and my testy thoughts for the rest of the day. And then I chewed on my thoughts some more. And then I really sat with my feelings and looked them in the face and came to the conclusion that my anger was really masking something deeper: shame. Her criticism of the broader conversation was valid, and so was her response to my comment on it.

I was ashamed that I hadn't noticed how ridiculous this debate about platform might be for women of color. I was ashamed I hadn't realized the differences between our two realities when it comes to book writing and blogging and conference speaking. I was ashamed I had fallen into the tired trap of thinking, *I'm not like that! I "get it," because I have a black daughter and a black best friend and other black friends.* I was ashamed because I had grown used to pointing my finger at others and didn't like having someone else point a finger at me.

I quietly looked myself in the soul and admitted, *Lauren, you are a hypocrite. You have more to learn than you realize. You are being a coward.* I didn't like being called out, but I needed to be called out. It was uncomfortable but necessary. Without fanfare or comment, I left the Twitter conversation . . . for several months. I shut my mouth and opened my ears. I listened and read and observed and learned, which was (and is) necessary. But to be perfectly frank, my initial response—leaving the conversation—was prompted as much by avoidance as it was self-awareness. It was me grabbing my ball and running home because I didn't like the way it felt when my wrist got slapped. The criticism felt unfair because I didn't initially see it for what it was: part of my sanctification process and, honestly, a gracious gift.

A crucial part of growing in love and cultivating empathy is the ability to receive critical feedback. How else will we know if our words and actions are helping or hurting others? How can we see the impact we have on others if we aren't willing to listen when they give voice to it? True harmony doesn't come from eliminating disagreement; it comes from listening, learning, and growing together through it. It comes from iron sharpening iron (Proverbs 27:17). It comes from allowing ourselves to be forged and reshaped in the hot pounding of the process. It may not be comfortable, but it is necessary. As Robin DiAngelo writes in her book *White Fragility*, "The key to moving forward is what we do with our discomfort. We can use it as a door out—blame the messenger and disregard the message. Or we can use it as a door in by asking, Why does this unsettle me? What would it mean for me [for us] if this were true?"[2]

❧

The 2016 US presidential election was one that put a hot spotlight on the deep and bitter divides that increasingly characterize our country. Two days after the election, I posted a lengthy status update on my public Facebook page. Here is a portion of it:

> Please do not tell me not to cry or grieve. Please do not tell your neighbors not to cry and grieve. Crying is a normal, healthy response to pain and fear and trauma. I make

myself stronger and smarter when I own my emotions. I work harder and love deeper when I allow myself, and others, to feel. Don't begrudge anyone that.

Christian friends, yes, I know that Jesus is still on the throne. I take great comfort in that. But I would remind you of a few things:

1. Jesus wept (John 11:35).
2. Ecclesiastes 3:4 tells me that there is "a time to weep, and a time to laugh; a time to mourn, and a time to dance."
3. There is an entire book of the Bible titled Lamentations.

I want to reach out to my friends who don't understand my reaction to the results of this election. I know you might be feeling very different than I do today, and I am honestly glad for you that you have no reason to feel grief or fear in the wake of this election. I mean that from the bottom of my heart. I want that for all people. I will not lash out against you or my neighbors, but simply ask that we all take the time to listen. It's the only thing that can bring unity and peace.[3]

Most of the comments that followed were understanding, but one woman took great issue with the fact that I wasn't celebrating as she was. She had been following me for years and assumed I would feel the same way she did. When it appeared that I did not, she was confused, but not rude. We had a civil exchange about the differences in our views, and because our comments were made in a public forum, another of my readers jumped in with her perspective. This reader was a passionate mixture of anger, fear, and grief. She was blunt but respectful, and I appreciated her input. The first woman, however, did not appreciate this woman's feedback and immediately went on the defensive. Over and over, she claimed she was being "attacked" when she was disagreed with. I tried to explain that no one was attacking her, just sharing a different viewpoint. I also tried to gently point out why some of the views and policies she was so vocally supportive of were causing real harm to people.

Even though we didn't agree, I thought the conversation was productive and good, but she announced that she was done—with the conversation and with me. In a final comment, she let me know she'd be unfollowing and said, "I don't have time for this right now. I have pumpkin spice bars to make."

Criticism, when it takes the form of honest feedback, rarely feels good, but it is necessary for growth and transformation. If we run away, declare ourselves too busy or too sensitive to be bothered by it, our lives and relationships will stagnate, and our efforts to make change will ring hollow. Sometimes we may be subject to unfair criticism, and when that happens, I hope we have the patience and maturity to filter it through the sieve of our hearts, taking what is good and true and helpful and tossing the rest. More often than not, criticism is an invitation to learn and grow and consider life from another's perspective. Comfort isn't peace, and criticism isn't persecution—in fact, it can be a sign of great love. We can learn to receive it as such.

When Jesus spoke about his imminent suffering, death, and resurrection, his disciples weren't thrilled with what they heard. Peter was aghast and protested, "This will never happen to you!" (Matthew 16:22 NLT). In other words, *this is unacceptable—it must never happen!*

Peter's intentions were good—to protect and defend—but they were also misguided. So Jesus called him out. It was a pretty harsh rebuke too. "Get away from me, Satan! You are a dangerous trap to me. You are seeing things merely from a human point of view, not from God's" (Matthew 16:23 NLT).

*Oof.* That had to land like a punch to the gut. But Jesus didn't send Peter away, and Peter didn't run away. In fact, Peter messed up a lot and was consistently rebuked by Jesus, but he took each correction to heart. As a result, he grew more loving and faithful and passionate and committed. Jesus wasn't attacking Peter; he was lovingly preparing him for a life of ministry.

When Jesus rebuked his disciples for shooing children away from him, he was showing them how to love. When he corrected them for rejecting the woman who anointed him with costly oil, he was showing them how to worship. When he told Martha that Mary had chosen the better way, he was showing her how to learn. Consistently throughout the Gospels, we see a Jesus who isn't stingy with his criticisms but uses them to help his followers become new people who see things in new ways—ways that sowed more seeds of love and empathy in the world.

I must consistently check my heart and mind to avoid falling into the same trap Pumpkin Spice Bar Lady fell into. I can choose how I receive criticism. One option is to step out of the spotlight that illuminates my flaws and failures. The other is to allow criticism to be a flashlight shining on a previously unseen experience, illuminating my path, and leading me forward into greater love and empathy.

※

I was in high school when my father rebuked me in a way that has stuck with me ever since. The conversation leading up to it had something to do with social groups and homecoming or prom. My sister, a college student at the time, said something snarky, and I retorted, "That's because I actually have friends." Even at the time, I knew it was brattier and meaner than whatever it was she'd said to me. My dad, sitting nearby, said in a stern voice, "Lauren, don't talk to your sister that way. You're better than that."

I can't adequately describe the way his words made me feel, because I'd never felt that way before. It was a weird mixture of sadness and disappointment in myself while simultaneously feeling incredibly loved by my dad. It was a rebuke that stung, to be sure, but my dad hadn't said, "*Be* better," he'd said, "You *are* better." He acknowledged the worst of what I'd done, but he did so by appealing to the best of who I was. I understood that he believed I already possessed everything I needed to act in a caring and compassionate manner. He corrected me, but he didn't shame me. I didn't see it that way at the time, though.

At the time my inner monologue was something like, *How unfair! He always takes her side.* [He didn't.] *And didn't he hear what she said to me? Why didn't he tell her to stop?* Then I probably rolled my eyes and stomped off to my room.

That exchange happened almost twenty years ago, but I still remember the impact his words had on me as if it were yesterday—and his words still feel incredibly loving. They push me to be kinder, more loving, and gentler in my own words. When I am criticized or rebuked, pride can push me to believe I'm being persecuted, but humility and love usually reveal areas for growth, for being more considerate of others—and if I stay with the discomfort long enough, I'm thankful for it. This is how we can allow criticism to increase our empathy.

❧

Even when we commit to a life of loving our neighbors, we're going to mess up. We'll reach out with good intentions only to find our outstretched hands slapped away because our love felt like anything but. Like when we, faced with a racist incident, reach out to comfort with words like, "Love is color-blind!" and are met with an emphatic "No, it isn't, and please don't say that!" Do we receive the criticism as a gift showing us how to truly love our neighbors with skin a darker hue than our own? Or do we tuck our hands in our pockets and sulk back home, wounded and jaded? Do we allow criticism to be our personal trainer, strengthening us to do it better the next time, or do we defend our fragility by walking away?

Receiving criticism well, as uncomfortable as it may feel, would guide us to seek to know why our words, meant in love, brought more harm. We would learn that "color blindness" simply erases the experiences, cultures, and beauty of those who aren't light skinned. Criticism, when accepted, opens our eyes and shows us how to love well because it leads us to empathy.

Anything worth doing will sooner or later attract criticism, and radical neighbor love is no exception. If we run away, declare ourselves too busy or too sensitive to engage it, we'll never learn how our own words and actions impact the people around us. Comfort is an idol, a false one that promises a false harmony. We must refuse to worship it. We need to name our feelings of being attacked or called out for what they truly are: discomfort. Then we need to be willing to follow where that discomfort leads us.

Let's strengthen our resolve, take the gift of criticism—absorbing what we need to change and grow, releasing what isn't true or fruitful—and continue moving toward our neighbors with love.

# SEVENTEEN

# HOPEFULLY EVER AFTER

Oft hope is born when all is forlorn.

J.R.R. TOLKIEN, *THE RETURN OF THE KING*

One evening five years ago, I ran into Walmart to grab a few things for our dinner while John and the kids waited in the car. Just like I did on many other ordinary evenings, after rushing through the aisles, I made my way to the self-checkout. As I was loading my bags into my cart, I heard soft voices just a few feet away. Turning to look, I found two little boys hovered over a candy display. They were turning the bags over in their hands and talking to one another about it, their faces an inch apart. Something about the back of their heads was just so familiar, so I stood there watching for a moment. Then one of the boys turned around.

The air sucked out of my lungs and my heart pounded

in my chest as I felt a mixture of elation and searing pain. I was staring at the face of one of our foster sons. I hadn't seen that precious face for nearly seven years, but it was the same little face, just on a much taller body. I stood there frozen, memorizing everything about him, and then his twin brother turned around. Heart pounding, I stared back and forth from one to the other. There they were, the boys I'd loved every single day for the last seven years, standing less than five feet from me. I was breathless. And then their gaze met mine.

I smiled softly and silently begged them to recognize me as I looked into their eyes. Two blank stares met my gaze. Nothing. My heart broke a little as I realized they didn't know me anymore. How could they, though? They were two and a half when they left my arms . . . but in this moment in Walmart, they were closing in on their ninth birthday. Still, I had hoped. These were the boys I had rocked to sleep every night for eighty-seven nights. I had kissed their boo-boos and wiped their tears. When they got sick, I'd wrapped them in blankets and held them close. We laughed and splashed at bath time; we picnicked in the mountains. I was there when they first saw the ocean. Now I was a stranger in Walmart.

Their father finished checking out behind me and called to the boys. They quickly dropped the candy bags and followed their dad. I grabbed my cart and hurried behind them. Once outside, I stood and watched as they half-skipped, half-trotted down the sidewalk to the other side of the parking lot. The joy I felt at seeing them quickly melted into grief as they faded from view. It was over in a blink—one minute they were there and the next they were gone. Again.

As they rounded the corner, I was transported back to seven years earlier. They were just two little boys wearing two little backpacks, half-skipping, half-trotting to the social services van. Through my tears I buckled them in. One looked up at me and said, "It's okay! Jesus with me when I go bye-bye car." The van pulled away while John and I stood weeping in the front yard. That had been the last moment I saw them.

As they disappeared from view once more, I stood outside Walmart with tears streaming down my cheeks, whispering to myself those sweet little words, "It's okay. Jesus with me when I go bye-bye . . ."

Life isn't perfect, and neither was the ending to my story with the twins. I would do it all over again, though, because in this broken world, the thing that brings me back to hope is the way we love one another. Every story doesn't get wrapped up in a pretty little bow, but we can wrap our arms around each other in the midst of the brokenness. And the simple act of seeing and caring for one another is enough to spark a flame of hope that can consume the world. Acts of empathy are declarations of hope—the belief that things can and will be better.

When John and I signed up to become foster parents in our community, it was driven by empathy born from our own heartbreak. After years of infertility, two devastating miscarriages, and conclusive evidence of our shared infertility, our dreams and expectations of what family would look like for us were dashed. But as we came out of the fog of our grief over things not being the way they were supposed to be, we lifted our gaze and began to examine our world to see we weren't the only ones hurting over family not being the way it was supposed to be.

We became aware of the children caught up in cycles of abuse, addiction, and extreme poverty in our community. Children who should have been going to bed with full bellies, full hearts, and sweet dreams were instead experiencing the gnawing pangs of hunger in the middle of the night, changing their own diapers, and wincing beneath the butts of cigarettes being snuffed out on their bare skin. John and I looked at each other and decided that things could be different. We dared to hope.

The paperwork process wasn't too difficult, and after some background checks, a home study, some classes, and fingerprint scans, we were approved to be foster parents. The phone call came on an April afternoon as I was heading out the front door to do some yard work. Our social worker's voice came through with a short and simple question: "There are twin two-year-old boys who need a safe home. I know you said you only felt up to take one child at a time, but would you consider taking in twins?"

It's really not hard to make a decision like this when you put yourself in the shoes of the children caught up in a mess they didn't make. John and I had a home with two extra bedrooms and a large bathtub that never got used. We had a kitchen full of food and a backyard full of grass. Our only hesitation was over fears that we would be in over our heads with more than one child, but when faced with actual need, those fears no longer seemed a valid excuse. Just a few hours later the boys were standing in our living room.

The thing about foster parenting is that it's an act of

hope from start to finish. Foster parents know going in that they will say goodbye to the children they fall in love with. We knew that the twins weren't ours to keep but ours to love—with our hands and feet for a time and our hearts for a lifetime—with the belief that it would make a difference, that it would matter. We might not be able to change the circumstances and environment that led to their home being an unsafe place, but we could provide a safe place, words of affirmation, and a gentle touch in the middle of a tumultuous and confusing time.

Hidden behind every peanut butter and jelly sandwich, every silly and fun bubble bath, every bedtime story and lullaby, is hope. Hope that these small moments will add up in the hearts and minds and bodies of the children in our care. And hope that if and when we are hurt and frightened, lonely and forgotten, someone will see us and stop the hustle and bustle of their lives to care for us. This kind of hope is driven by empathy, and it's the reason any of us bother to care and love our neighbors in the midst of an upside-down, messed-up, inside-out world at all. Because we believe it matters. Because we have hope.

So that first night we bathed the boys, gently gliding over bruises and scars with warm water and bubbles. We rubbed Johnson & Johnson lavender bedtime lotion into their skin and pulled fresh, new pajamas over their heads. We tucked them into a warm bed, read them a story, and sang the few lullabies we could remember before turning out the lights. When cries rang out in the middle of the night, I found myself cross-legged on the floor, rocking the body of a child I'd only just met, praying for sleep and peace.

In the weeks that followed, we fell into a routine. Legos scattered across our living room floor and board books piled up on the coffee table. We learned that bananas were a favorite but tomatoes were not. Motorcycles and lawn mowers would elicit shouts of joy, but the bath was still scary. We took a walk around the neighborhood every evening and visited the playground most days. Day by day we saw them relax into the safety of our home. Their bruises faded along with the dark circles under their eyes. Their cheeks grew round and pink, and their eyes grew brighter. We saw healing happening before our very eyes, so when the call came that the boys were to return home less than three months later, we struggled.

John and I desperately wanted to know that the boys would be okay, that their home had been transformed into a safe place for them to live and grow and thrive. With no such assurances, we didn't quite know how to feel now that our time with them had ended. Several times in the weeks that followed their leaving, I caught myself wondering, *What was the point of that?* Remembering the struggle in the wake of the twins' departure reminds me of a recent conversation I had with Mareto.

"Being kind doesn't work," he announced during bedtime not too long ago. Despondent about failed efforts to turn classmates into friends, he wanted to give up. I understand. Too many times I've wanted to throw in the towel myself. What's the point of kindness if nothing ever changes? What's the point of empathy if it doesn't change the trajectory of humanity? Playground kids are still mean. Some people still choose evil over good, wrong over right. There is death and disease, fire and flood. While some people starve, others devour everything in their paths. Loved ones have cancer, friends lose jobs, nations go to war, and little boys return to unsafe homes. Like my son, I can be tempted to give up, to believe empathy doesn't work.

Except that it does.

And so I give myself the same daily pep talk I give to my children: "It works. It matters. It makes a difference. Don't give up. It really does change things, even when we can't see it."

One of the most frustrating things about life is, we don't always get to see the fruit of our labor—but this doesn't mean our labor is fruitless. Empathy leads us to love, and it is always a worthwhile endeavor. Empathy is a journey and love is the destination, and the span of our lives is the time it takes to get from here to there.

So we pack the school lunches and read bedtime stories and wait in the school drop-off line with a smile and wave to the parents around us. We sit together in the waiting room at rehab in grief and fear, hanging on to tattered threads of hope. We write letters to incarcerated loved ones believing that they were made for more. We keep showing up on our neighbor's doorstep offering coffee and a hug. We keep listening and learning, inviting and forgiving; we keep sharing and amplifying voices and stepping outside of our comfort zones. We rest when we're weary and then make sure our neighbors have the same opportunity. We worship together and laugh together and cry together and keep striving to see one another. Not because we'll fix the world and always get to see the results of our labor, but because it's the only way to live a life of love.

Archbishop Desmond Tutu expressed this sentiment beautifully when addressing the people working for peace in Belfast, Ireland:

> What each of us does can retard or promote, can hinder or advance the process at the heart of the universe. Christians would say the outcome is not in question. The death and resurrection of Jesus Christ puts the issue beyond doubt: ultimately goodness and laughter and peace and compassion and gentleness and forgiveness and reconciliation will have the last word and prevail over their ghastly counterparts.[1]

Every year on Ash Wednesday, I am reminded of my mortality and my need for Jesus. I remember the pastors of my youth dipping their fingers in bowls of ash, lifting them to my forehead, and reciting over me, "From dust you came, to dust you will return," as they marked a gray cross on my forehead. A beginning and an end. Life wrapped up in a cindered bow. I think about where we came from and where we're going, and I can't help but see beyond the ashes.

We came from the dust of Eden. We were shaped and formed and molded by the hands of a God who is perfect peace, joy, justice, and love. He placed all of that in and around us and called it good. We were made by him, made for him, and made in his own image. Then it all fell apart. We left Eden and got a little lost, wandering through the in-between, searching for home. God, in his perfect grace and mercy, wrapped all his peace, joy, justice, and love in skin and gave us his son, Jesus. Hope in the flesh. "Follow me," he said, as he showed us the way back to love.

The in-between—the interval between where we came from and where we're going—may be long, hard, and painful, but we started from perfect love and to perfect love we will return. So, we press on, hopefully ever after.

# MAY WE WALK IN LOVE

Let me give you a new command: Love one another. In
the same way I loved you, you love one another. This is
how everyone will recognize that you are my disciples—
when they see the love you have for each other.
JOHN 13:34–35, THE MESSAGE

Today I pray for us. All of us. You, me, your kids and mine.
Our bosses, our parents, our siblings, our neighbors, our
in-laws. Our pastors, our teachers, our leaders, our friends.

I pray that we would see. God, open our eyes to the world
around us—the bustling, busy, ever-moving and changing,
sometimes thriving, often hurting world around us. Free us
from the scales that cover our eyes, just as you freed Saul
from his on the road to Damascus. Remove the obstacles
that blind us and keep us from really seeing one another as
we are—as you made us.

Let us remember that every person on earth was created in your image, God. May we see each other as you see

us—your children. Help us to stop assigning value and worth based on earthly things like money and power and outside appearances. Show us who we keep missing and pushing to the margins. Make us notice those who are all too often hidden from view.

From the CEO to the worker in the assembly line. From the lead pastor to the gay child who left the pews. From the senators and governors to the homeless who line the streets of the communities they represent. From the preschoolers to the elderly. From the exhausted mother to the insecure teenager. From the addict in rehab to the drug dealer in prison. From the soldiers lining the borders to the children washing up on our shores. Let us see you in them and our role in their stories. Give us eyes to see, Lord.

I pray that we would understand. May we dig deeper to uncover the truth behind the broken systems and relationships and structures of this world. May we quit shrugging our shoulders or turning our backs and instead seek to learn. When faced with perspectives that don't fit our own narratives, show us how to take the harder but more worthwhile path of seeking answers rather than the easier route of dismissal. Teach us to reject ignorance and love truth and knowledge.

You have given us so many treasures on earth, so many ways to know and grow from the experiences of others. Guide us to every book, every podcast, every speech, every organization, every relationship that would increase our understanding of each other and the world around us. Remind us to ask "why?" and "what if?" on a regular basis. Cultivate in us an active imagination and a thirst for discovery. Shut our mouths and open our minds. Give us ears to hear, Lord.

I pray that we would feel. You have made us so much more than a robotic system of nerves and blood vessels and bones and muscle. You have breathed life into our souls just as surely as your breath sustains our bodies. Do not let our hearts become numb in the face of ongoing tragedy, loss, and evil. Give us courage and strength to face the things that scare us because they ignite overwhelming emotion. Let us not be afraid to feel with our fellow travelers on this journey of life.

Our culture might shame tears, but you've assured us that you keep and treasure every last one of them, Lord. Teach us to sit and weep with one another as you did with Mary and Martha when their brother Lazarus died. Show us how to share in each other's joys and sorrows with vulnerability and grace. May we wear our hearts on our sleeves and invite others to do the same. Give us hearts that break, Lord.

I pray that we would act. Let empathy lead us toward a life of service, not born from paternalism but sisterhood and brotherhood. May we dive headlong into our neighborhoods ready to get our hands dirty. Give us strength and mercy as we follow you into the lives of our neighbors. When we don't know what to do, show us.

Help us be brave enough to go big. To preach the sermon that scares us, to write the book that is born from sweat and tears, to start the nonprofit, to storm the halls of congress, to demand justice, to march for freedom, to flip tables and speak truth to power.

Remind us that there is no act of love too small to

matter. That it sometimes looks like baking a casserole for the sick friend and dropping off coffee for the tired mom down the street. Or sending flowers to the funeral home and quietly cleaning the dishes in the kitchen while the bereaved family laughs and reminisces. Or giving each other rides to work when the car breaks down and sitting in silence with a hurting loved one. Or calling our friend and asking for forgiveness. Writing letters to the deployed and visiting the incarcerated. Mowing the lawn of the disabled veteran across town. Filling each other's refrigerators with food, homes with laughter and tears, and hearts with prayer. Give us hands to serve, Lord.

You have commanded us to love, and you've already shown us how. Help us to see one another, to understand each other, to feel with our brothers and sisters. May we walk in love.

Amen.

# ACKNOWLEDGMENTS

This part of finishing up a manuscript feels so daunting because I am convinced I am going to forget someone, or many someones, who have aided in this process in big and small ways. That is most certainly going to happen, so let me cover my bases right now and say thank you to any and all who have crossed my path in life. My interactions with others have shaped my worldview and fed my drive to write. Now here I am, putting the final touches on my second book. Truly, thank you.

To John, thank you for never giving up on yourself, on me, and on us. You are always in my corner, and I don't thank you enough for that. Thank you for believing in me, seeing the best in me, and encouraging my dreams. I'm so grateful I get to do life with you . . . for better or worse . . . forever. I love you.

To Mareto and Arsema, you are the delight of my life. Pieces of me came alive when I became your mother, and I never knew I had so much fire in me until you ignited it in the best possible ways. I see you and I love you. I will always be here for you with open arms . . . no. matter. what.

To my parents, thank you for being proud of me. Thank you for believing in and seeing the best in me. Thank you for being a safe place to land whenever I need you. You've put in overtime the last few years, and it hasn't gone unnoticed or unappreciated. I love you.

To Rachel, you have been listening to me ramble on about this book for years. You've been there for the fiery rants and the tear-filled confessions and concerns. You've met each moment of writer's block with the firm encouragement to just keep going. You've kept me sane with memes about our favorite duchess (Sussex forever!) and hilarious work stories. I love you, my person.

To the many authors, artists, reporters, journalists, historians, theologians, activists, advocates, musicians, and writers who have given the world their time and talents to uplift the marginalized, unheard, oppressed, and dismissed, I thank you. I have learned so much from you. You've widened the lens through which I view humanity and history. You've increased my empathy and expanded my capacity for neighbor love. This book simply wouldn't exist without me partaking of the fruits of your labor.

To Rachel Held Evans, who passed away during the editing phase of this book, I learned so much from you, not the least of which is to be brave about telling the truth. Thank you for giving so much of yourself to the world while you were here. Eshet Chayil. Woman of Valor. You are missed. Your memory is a blessing. You will not be forgotten.

To Lisa, my longsuffering and endlessly patient agent, thank you for being my writing coach, counselor, cheerleader, and friend. You are someone I trust with my hopes, dreams, disappointments, and victories. Thank you for being there for me.

To Jessica, my equally longsuffering and endlessly patient editor, thank you for taking my words and helping them make sense. You push me to be a better writer. Thank you for believing in me and my message. You are a kindred spirit, and I wish we lived closer so we could watch *You've Got Mail* together every autumn.

To the wonderful team at Thomas Nelson, thank you for championing my writing. It takes a huge team to make a book like this come to life—from book cover design, to marketing and sales and copyediting, and every little bit in between—thank you so much for all your hard work and passion.

To my readers, thank you for supporting my work. No, really. You have no idea how much it means to me that of all the books in the world you chose to read this one. I would be out of a job without you, so thank you from the bottom of my heart.

# NOTES

## INTRODUCTION

1. "Towards a Global Ethic: An Initial Declaration," Wikipedia, last updated May 27, 2019, https://en.wikipedia.org/wiki/Towards_a_Global_Ethic:_An_Initial_Declaration.
2. Editorial Committee of the Council of the Parliament of the World's Religions, "Declaration Toward a Global Ethic," Parliament of the World's Religions, September 1993, https://parliamentofreligions.org/pwr_resources/_includes/FCKcontent/File/TowardsAGlobalEthic.pdf, 1–2.

## CHAPTER 1: THE ANTIDOTE TO INDIFFERENCE

1. Editorial Committee of the Council of the Parliament of the World's Religions, "Declaration toward a Global Ethic," Parliament of the World's Religions, September 1993, https://parliamentofreligions.org/pwr_resources/_includes/FCKcontent/File/TowardsAGlobalEthic.pdf, 1.
2. *You've Got Mail*, directed by Nora Ephron (Burbank, CA: Warner Bros., 1998).

## CHAPTER 2: WE ALL FALL DOWN

1. World Vision Staff, "2017 Hurricane Harvey: Facts, FAQs, and How to Help," World Vision, last updated September 7,

2018, https://www.worldvision.org/disaster-relief-news
-stories/2017-hurricane-harvey-facts.

2. Monte Plott, "Cajun Navy Brings Boats from Louisiana to
   Help Flood-Ravaged Houston," CNN, August 29, 2017,
   https://www.cnn.com/2017/08/29/us/harvey-cajun-navy
   /index.html.

## CHAPTER 3: BLIND SPOTS

1. *Friends*, season 2, episode 5, "The One with Five Steaks and
   an Eggplant," directed by Ellen Gittelsohn, written by David
   Crane et al., aired October 19, 1995, on NBC, https://www
   .amazon.com/One-Five-Steaks-Eggplant/dp/B000KZFMZI/.

## CHAPTER 4: BORN FOR OTHERS

1. Stephen Holden, "After a Struggle to Escape Comes an
   Effort to Adjust," January 12, 2007, *New York Times*,
   https://www.nytimes.com/2007/01/12/movies/12tire.html.

2. *God Grew Tired of Us*, written and directed by Christopher
   Quinn (Washington D.C.: National Geographic Films,
   2007), https://www.amazon.com/God-Grew-Tired-Nicole
   -Kidman/dp/B078WWHBYL/.

3. Andrea Perkins, "'Lost Boys' Share Thoughts After Film,"
   *Pittsburgh Post-Gazette*, April 10, 2008, https://www.post
   -gazette.com/local/east/2008/04/10/lost-boys-share
   -thoughts-after-film/stories/200804100490.

## CHAPTER 5: TUNING OUR HEARTS TO THE STORIES AROUND US

1. Austin Channing Brown, *I'm Still Here: Black Dignity in a
   World Made for Whiteness* (New York: Convergent Books,
   2018), 107–109.

2. For more information, visit www.facebook.com/groups
   /BetheBridge.

3. Trevor Noah, *Born a Crime: Stories from a South African
   Childhood* (New York: Spiegel & Grau, 2016), 193–95.

## CHAPTER 6: THE MAGIC OF *WHAT IF?*

1. Brendan Gaesser, "Constructing memory, imagination, and empathy: a cognitive neuroscience perspective," *Frontiers in Psychology*, January 9, 2013, https://www.frontiersin.org /articles/10.3389/fpsyg.2012.00576/full.

2. Alexander Koch, et al., "Earth System Impacts of the European Arrival and Great Dying in the Americas after 1492," *Quaternary Science Reviews*, vol. 207, March 2019, https://www.sciencedirect.com/science/article/pii /S0277379118307261#.

## CHAPTER 7: BIG FEELINGS LEAD TO BIG LOVE

1. *Won't You Be My Neighbor?* directed by Morgan Neville (New York: Focus Features, 2018), http://www .focusfeatures.com/wont-you-be-my-neighbor/.

2. Lauren Casper, *It's Okay About It: Lessons from a Remarkable Five-Year-Old About Living Life Wide Open* (Nashville, TN: Nelson Books, 2017), 12–13.

## CHAPTER 8: SCARLET LETTERS AND STRINGS OF PEARLS

1. Andre Henry, "To All the White Friends I Couldn't Keep," AndreRHenry.com, February 5, 2019, http://www .andrerhenry.com/thoughts/2019/2/5/to-all-the-white -friends-i-couldnt-keep.

## CHAPTER 9: STRANGERS ARE JUST NEIGHBORS WE HAVEN'T MET YET

1. Brendan Gaesser, "Constructing memory, imagination, and empathy: a cognitive neuroscience perspective," *Frontiers in Psychology*, January 9, 2013, https://www.frontiersin.org /articles/10.3389/fpsyg.2012.00576/full.

2. To read Dr. King's speech, see "Address at the Conclusion of the Selma to Montgomery March," The Martin Luther King, Jr. Research and Education Institute, March 25, 1965,

https://kinginstitute.stanford.edu/king-papers/documents
/address-conclusion-selma-montgomery-march. To watch
Rev. Dr. Barber's speech delivered on January 27, 2019, at
Washington and Lee University, see "MLK Legacy Week
Keynote Address with Rev. Dr. William Barber, II" on
YouTube.com, starting at 1:09:53: https://www.youtube
.com/watch?v=u44sBkPDtPc.

3. To learn more about Project Connection, visit their website,
projectconnectionpc.org.

## CHAPTER 10: THE NEXT RIGHT THING

1. To read the Gospel accounts of this encounter, see Matthew
9:18–22, Mark 5:25–34, and Luke 8:43–48.

2. To learn more about Lucy McBath's story, see John
Verhovek and Meg Cunningham, "Lucy McBath wins
seat in Congress, was inspired to run in the wake of
Parkland and after losing son to gun violence," ABC News,
November 8, 2018, https://abcnews.go.com/Politics
/losing-son-gun-violence-wake-parkland-lucy-mcbath
/story?id=58966402.

## CHAPTER 11: YOURS, MINE, OURS

1. "Haiti quake death toll rises to 230,000," BBC News,
February 11, 2010, http://news.bbc.co.uk/2/hi/americas
/8507531.stm.

## CHAPTER 12: THE BUDDY BENCH

1. Glennon Doyle, Facebook, June 5, 2014, https://www
.facebook.com/glennondoyle/photos/a.213343589709/10156
426421424710/?type=1&theater.

## CHAPTER 13: FOUR HUNDRED AND NINETY TIMES MORE

1. Jemar Tisby, The Color of Compromise (Grand Rapids, MI:
Zondervan, 2019), 14.

2. Ibid., 15.

3. John Paul Brammer, "Mama Tammye of Queer Eye Has a Message for Queer People That Will Make You Sob," Them, August 13, 2018, https://www.them.us/story/tammye -queer-eye-qa.

4. Mary Bowerman and Ashley May, "Martin Luther King, Jr. quotes: 10 most popular from the civil rights leader," *USA Today*, January 21, 2019, https://www.usatoday.com/story /news/nation/2019/01/21/martin-luther-king-jr-quotes-10 -most-popular/2636024002/.

## CHAPTER 14: THE INTERNET IS STILL REAL LIFE

1. Elisha Fieldstadt, "Patton Oswalt helps man who trolled him on Twitter raise $30,000 for medical bills," NBC News, January 25, 2019, https://www .nbcnews.com/pop-culture/pop-culture-news/patton -oswalt-helps-man-who-trolled-him-twitter-raise- 30-n962706.

2. Bana Alabed (@AlabedBana), 2016, "Good afternoon from #Aleppo I'm reading to forget the war," Twitter, September 26, 2016, 4:27 a.m., https://twitter.com/AlabedBana/status /780368067675230208.

3. Michael Andor Brodeur, "Online, Empathy Adapts to Survive," *Boston Globe*, October 9, 2016, https://www .bostonglobe.com/lifestyle/2016/10/09/online-empathy -adapts-survive/lzjcF4cZygQ9qmrVsDiNYI/story.html.

## CHAPTER 15: PASS THE MIC

1. To learn more about the Autistic Self Advocacy Network (ASAN), visit their website, autisticadvocacy.org.

2. Sarah Bessey, "Why We Don't Need 'Women's' Ministry," Church Leaders, May 7, 2015, https://churchleaders.com /pastors/pastor-articles/155219-sarah-bessey-why-women -s-ministry-needs-jesus.html.

## CHAPTER 16: COMFORT VS. CRITICISM

1. Elbert Hubbard, *Little Journeys to the Homes of the Great, Memorial Edition* (New York: Wm. Wise & Co., Inc., 1916), 370.
2. Robin DiAngelo, *White Fragility* (Boston: Beacon Press, 2018), 14.
3. Lauren Casper, Facebook, November 10, 2016, https://www.facebook.com/LaurenCasperDotCom/posts/1822235671394035,

## CHAPTER 17: HOPEFULLY EVER AFTER

1. Desmond Tutu, *No Future Without Forgiveness* (New York: Doubleday, 1999), 267.

# ABOUT THE AUTHOR

Lauren Casper is a writer, speaker, advocate, and amateur baker. She is the founder of the popular blog lauren-casper.com and has had numerous articles syndicated by the *Huffington Post*, the *TODAY Show*, Yahoo! News, and several other publications. Lauren and her husband, John, have two beautiful children and one fluffy dog. They make their home in the Shenandoah Valley of Virginia.